ALL that *MATTERS*

To the fond memory of George MacLeod,
Founder of the Iona Community
to whom
matter mattered

ALL that *MATTERS*

Scripts from BBC Radio 4's 'Thought for the Day'
and other musings

John L. Bell

WILD GOOSE PUBLICATIONS
www.ionabooks.com

First published 2010 by
Wild Goose Publications, Fourth Floor, Savoy House,
140 Sauchiehall Street, Glasgow G2 3DH, UK,
the publishing division of the Iona Community.
Scottish Charity No. SC003794.
Limited Company Reg. No. SC096243.

ISBN 978-1-84952-070-6

Cover Graham Maule © 2010 WGRG, Iona Community,
Glasgow G2 3DH

A catalogue record for this book is available from the British Library.

Overseas distribution
Australia: Willow Connection Pty Ltd, Unit 4A,
3-9 Kenneth Road, Manly Vale, NSW 2093.
New Zealand: Pleroma, Higginson Street,
Otane 4170, Central Hawkes Bay.

Permission to reproduce any part of this work in Australia
or New Zealand should be sought from Willow Connection.

Printed by Bell & Bain, Thornliebank, Glasgow

Mixed Sources
Product group from well-managed
forests and other controlled sources
www.fsc.org Cert no. TT-COC-002769
© 1996 Forest Stewardship Council

Contents

Introduction

This is the second collection of scripts most of which were first voiced in the *Thought For the Day* slot at around 7.50 am on BBC Radio 4's *Today* programme. Such writing is necessarily ephemeral. Like the best of sermons, it is meant for one occasion, not for endless repetition, the more so since the BBC asks contributors to reflect on an issue of topical concern in the light of their espoused faith.

What is topical today may not be so tomorrow. Which should make such a collection of talks redundant, except that what is recorded here is an example of the perennial task of any Christian communicator, namely to enable belief in what is eternal to impinge on what is transient.

The kingdom of God, in Jesus' understanding, is a terrestrial reality. It is this world and this time which are meant for transformation. It is the here and now for which the magnificent dreams of God, the prophecies of Scripture, the demands of Christ are meant. This is not to deny the realm of the Spirit, the importance of prayer and the practice of personal devotion. Rather it is to ground faith in the real world and thus prevent it from becoming pious speculation.

As in the previous volume, *Thinking Out Loud*, there are a few extended articles which were first delivered as lectures. In these I have endeavoured, on a larger canvas, to deal with some of the issues which short *Thought For The Day* broadcasts cannot address in depth. There is, therefore, an inevitable but small amount of duplication.

To those who issued such invitations to lecture, as to the staff of the BBC Department of Religion, I am indebted. I make no claim to expertise either in current affairs or in academic theology. But I believe that because God made and loves the world, it is incumbent on those who believe themselves to be called to preach not to baulk at either contentious issues or difficult texts.

Faith is, after all, a process rather than a destination. I hope that this volume might help others along the way.

John L. Bell
May 2010

Acknowledgement

As ever I am indebted to Sandra Kramer, publishing manager of Wild Goose Publications, for her care and attention to detail in editing work intended for public utterance so that it is suitable for private reading; and to my colleague Graham Maule who for 25 years has ensured that everything we have published has appeared wearing interesting clothing.

The scripts

children

Moderating the media

Music evokes. It certainly did for me yesterday morning. I almost burned the toast when I heard a tune from my childhood, the theme music for the '60s news programme called *Tonight*, being played on *Today*.

But what prevented me from indulging in a reminiscence project was hearing Cliff Michelmore, the former *Tonight* presenter, saying that the programme had been initiated to fill the gap known as 'toddler time'. That was between 6 and 7 pm, when hitherto both television channels (there were only two in the '60s) took an hour off air to allow parents to get young children to bed.

What a contrast today when many households have access to hundreds of television channels and, more particularly, when according to recent research more than 50% of three-year-olds have a television set in their bedroom.

Now, I have to be careful when I talk about children. I don't have any and I cannot pretend to know what it feels like to be a father. But I subscribe to the belief that it takes a village, not just parents, to rear a child. And I hold to a faith in which Jesus was keen to protect children from being tainted by the world.

So I want to take seriously research such as that which appeared in a recent professional journal for biologists which indicates possible links between television viewing and attention deficit disorder, short-sightedness and obesity.

And I also want to listen for the voice of my grandmother who knew quite a lot about child-rearing. She used to say what a privilege it was to be with children in their early years because you saw a new thing every day. For her the novelty in a developing child was infinitely more important than a box in the bedroom showing endless distractions.

Every child is unique. If he or she is made in the image of God, then he or she is a one-off, and that uniqueness is not best nurtured either by the output of the mass media or by strict adherence to a textbook on childcare. Uniqueness is nurtured when parent and child talk, laugh, play, cuddle and do all the human relating things for which there are no mechanical substitutes.

It used to be a common maxim that parents made sacrifices for their children ... not just in terms of money but also of personal time and personal comfort, because sacrifice is a measure of love. But if, instead of parents seeing and celebrating a new thing in their child every day, television becomes a means of surrogate care, then maybe it is the child who is being expected to sacrifice his or her natural development so that the parents can have an easier life.

Today is Ash Wednesday. It marks the start of the season of Lent. In the past people were encouraged to give up something they were fond of during Lent. Now we are encouraged to take up something important ... which for some of us could be looking at and learning from our children.

21 Feb 07

demonisation

Resettling the offender

In the street of 52 council houses in which I grew up, there was a man who sexually abused his adolescent daughter, and who was imprisoned for the offence. His wife being dead, his children were looked after by relatives and he, after serving his time, came back to live in the same house.

There would have been around 20 children in that street between the ages of eight and twelve. We all knew each other, and we all knew what the man had done, but none of our parents, whatever they may have said to each other, demonised him before us.

He's a long time dead now, with no other offences to his name.

In the light of continual belligerence towards sex offenders, in no small way whipped up by the popular press, the resettlement of such a criminal in my hometown must seem grossly naive.

But, then, everybody knew him and that diminished any threat he posed. Besides, people then as now were aware that the vast majority of offences against children are committed by relatives ... though we have yet to see major newspaper campaigns warning mothers against the paedophilic potential in their brothers-in-law.

I would not be surprised if some of the most strident voices calling for sex offenders to be continually named and shamed after their prison sentence might belong to people, men especially, who protest loudly to detract from their own sense of guilt or even temptation.

I say that because there is a similar though not parallel situation depicted in the story of Jesus kneeling beside a woman who was caught in the act of adultery, and who, by the law of the day, was liable to be stoned to death.

Her accusers, all men brim-full of self-righteousness, were sadly discomfited when Jesus encouraged them to start the stoning, inviting the person who was guiltless to pitch the first boulder. They walked away, the eldest first.

Was that because they were all adulterers. Or because they knew within themselves the strength of allurement?

More than adulterers, paedophiles are prominently on the receiving end of society's opprobrium, partly because they are easy targets but also because parents rightly want to protect their children.

So, with regard to their reintegration into society, I find myself asking two questions. Firstly: does it make a community more secure if, in the name of safety, we cavalierly demonise and ostracise those who have served their time?

And secondly: If we subscribe to a society whose obsession with sexuality is the leitmotif of advertisements, chat shows, tabloids and satellite television, can we expect that suggestible people will never become perverse?

13 April 07

obstructing

Greater love has no one than this

In any massacre, such as that which befell Virginia Tech recently, there are always elements of the irrational. The most immediate for many will be why it happened. But I doubt whether the video posted to the media by the killer, Cho Seung-Hui, will be of much help in this respect. A long time ago the sociologist Emile Durkheim discovered that suicide notes do not always reveal the true motive, but may often be a distraction.

It would be a pity, however, if it were only the irrationality of Cho Seung-Hui's actions that remained a mystery. There is another mystery which deserves to be celebrated as much as the gunman deserves to be condemned.

When we talk of someone 'getting in the way', we are normally bemoaning a person's obstructiveness, not their heroism. But presumption of nuisance cannot be levelled against Liviu Librescu, also of Virginia Tech, not a student but a professor.

He, a holocaust survivor who fled his native Romania, became an aeronautics expert in the USA. He was teaching a class when Cho went on the rampage. He told his students to jump out of the window while he barricaded the door and then threw himself in the path of the attacker. A man of 76, he got in the way of a killer less than a third of his age, whom other lecturers were known to fear.

Mr Librescu was a Jew who died confronting someone not of

15

his faith, and in defence of students who did not all share his religion. It is important to say this if for no other reason than that it stands in blatant contradiction to any supposition that Jews, or indeed people of any faith community, are essentially protective only of their own kind.

One hopes that Mr Librescu will remain, for many who hear his story, an exemplar of that truth which a first-century Jew once celebrated in the words, 'There is no greater love than this: that a man should lay down his life for his friends.'

And I wonder, I just wonder, whether in a culture which so gauchely celebrates those who ruthlessly kick obstructers out of their way to fulfil personal ambition, the example of this man might encourage others to get in the way of whatever or whoever threatens humanity.

20 April 2007

women's experiences

Things a man cannot understand

'I'm afraid that my wife doesn't love me any more!' – that's what he said. That's what was worrying him.

His name was Robert. He was a manual labourer working near where I used to live. He was 25 and one of the most unexpectedly tender men I've ever met.

But he feared that his wife didn't love him any more. And he knew that it had something to do with how, a month previously, she had given birth to their second child, a girl who was stillborn.

I could have told him that the rate of stillbirths has been unchanged for ages. That was confirmed earlier this week by an enquiry into Maternal and Child Health. Despite advances in medicine, 1 in 200 pregnancies end in stillbirth, and 1 in 300 babies die before they are 4 weeks old. These statistics are not the stuff of common gossip. They are too painful and, for many expectant parents, too menacing to contemplate.

No, such information would not have been consoling to Robert. Nor would the comparison between now and 2000 years ago. For in the Middle East, at the time of Christ, at least 1 in 4 children died at birth, and of live births 1 in 3 were dead by the age of 6.

No. These figures would have been no consolation either.

So I had nothing to say by way of insight or experience to this lovely worried young man.

But as he spoke about what had transpired, something dawned on both of us at the same time, namely that he – as the father – was grieving for a relationship with his second child which could never begin. Whereas his wife, as the mother of a baby who had lived in her womb, was grieving for a relationship which had ended.

I don't remember the name of Robert's wife. But I always think of her as Hannah.

That's the name of a woman in the Hebrew scriptures who had a similar predicament. She, despite trying long and hard, had been unable to conceive.

Her plight was not understood by two important men in her life. Her husband presumed that his avowals of love would compensate for her deep anguish. Her priest, seeing her mumble senselessly, presumed she had taken to the bottle. Despite being a man of faith, he never thought she might be spilling out her heart to God.

Like Robert and many other men, Hannah's husband and her male priest had not considered that there may be some experiences a woman undergoes which a man just cannot understand … some experiences where silence and sensitivity have to displace presumption.

27 April 2007

a bigger world

The university of experience

Yesterday at a festival in Cheltenham I heard the Secretary of State for International Development answer endless questions from people interested in Britain's engagement with the Third World. He spoke with intelligence, conviction and compassion.

He's one of a number of British politicians, from across the political spectrum, who are committed to working for a fairer world and who, with the Prime Minister, share the pedigree of having a father who was a clergyman.

There are many disadvantages in being brought up in a vicarage or a manse, not least of which is the presumption of other people that you will automatically share every religious conviction espoused by your ordained parent. But on the plus side is the exposure from childhood to a belief that the world is bigger than the self, as well as an awareness that practical compassion is a supreme virtue.

I am not suggesting for a moment that every vicar's daughter is a Mother Teresa in waiting. Nor am I suggesting that Christian ministers produce the best politicians. I would much rather vote for a good MP who was a non-believer than for some paragon of piety who couldn't tell a white paper from a colour supplement.

What interests me is the effect in adult life of being raised in a household where the stuff of daily conversation includes the wider world in all its potential and horror, and where the experience of daily living exposes children to a range of people who are dissimilar from their immediate family.

This awareness from childhood of life beyond the concerns and confines of the family is not exclusive to clergy households. For the children of clergy it is a given. Other households, if they value the development of a social conscience in the young, may have to be more intentional in encouraging it.

I didn't grow up in a manse, but my parents, although comparatively poor, were keen to raise my brothers and me with an awareness of the bigger world.

When I was 11, we had to forgo a summer holiday so that, the next year, the whole family could travel to Germany. My father, who had been stationed near Cologne after the war, had kept contact with a German couple who had befriended him. He wanted us to know that the world was more than Scotland. And at a time when magazines for boys still vilified Germans, he was keen that we should meet such people as friends.

For my parents, being was more important than having; people were more important than things; social justice was more important than selfishness. Almost fifty years later I still bless them for that.

And I wonder what gift of broad experience given by parents today will be remembered with gratitude by their children tomorrow.

27 August 07

money

Financial disparity

Five or six years ago, I had dinner in Amsterdam with two bright young South African lawyers who had been recruited by Dutch firms.

In the course of our conversation, I asked whether they were in the kind of businesses where they might expect to receive substantial bonuses. They said they'd been told that if they wanted to receive golden handshakes they should go to London rather than come to the Netherlands.

But I pressed them, 'Supposing you became partners in your respective Dutch firms, would you never get a bonus at Christmas?'

'Yes,' they said, 'but just a little.'

'How much?' I asked.

'Perhaps €100,000.' they replied. At that time, €100,000 was the equivalent of £50,000.

'Tell me,' I continued, 'who do you think most deserves €100,000 at Christmas, you or the primary school teachers who enabled you to believe in yourselves?'

'Ah,' one of them retorted, 'but that's the public sector.'

... and there's the rub, and the perennial ethical dilemma.

Two weeks ago brought news that directors of leading companies in Britain had an average salary rise of 37% in the last year. Last week prison officers took strike action in protest against their staged 2.5% pay rise, and this week the TUC mooted the possibility of further public sector wage disputes.

The public sector workers have been told to buckle their belts, but the lack of directive to the top 10% in the private sphere could be taken as an incentive to expand their waistlines.

It's almost a Dives and Lazarus predicament … by which I refer to a story Jesus told about a rich man who cared nothing for the beggar who lived in close proximity. After death, the two were separated by a great chasm with poor Lazarus in heaven and rich Dives somewhere considerably hotter.

The point of Jesus' story was not to placate the poor with the promise of privilege in the afterlife, but to draw the attention of the wealthy to a social disorder which was of their own making.

While we cannot all earn the same wages, we can at least have parity of policy. For if a nation is prepared to restrict the earnings of those whose salaries it can immediately control, yet is reticent to address corporate greed, there is a clear lack of joined up ethical thinking.

I'm saying this because I'm concerned about religion inter-fering with politics. You see, if a nation wants to prevent that from happening, it should be careful not to encourage the lust for wealth which is tantamount to idolatry for the simple reason that idolatry is a form of religion, and money is an unstable god.

13 September 2007

debt

Of human bondage

The other day I found myself humming a Sunday School song I last sang about 50 years ago. The first line is:
   'The wise man built his house upon the rock.'

There are no prizes for guessing which disaster befalling a prestigious financial institution brought these words to mind in glorious irony.

The predicament in which the Northern Rock Building Society found itself is commonly attributed to the recent unwillingness of financial institutions to lend to each other, a situation now ameliorated by the intervention of the Chancellor and a decrease in US interest rates. But is the present financial malaise only due to restrictions in the money markets? Or might another contributory factor be the chicken and egg relationship between borrowing and lending which has spiralled on the domestic front?

People of my age may remember the mixed reaction in the 1950s and '60s that greeted wider public access to the 'Never Never' ... a popular expression for Hire Purchase or Deferred Payment.

My grandmother, who lived on the breadline during the Depression, detested Hire Purchase, and keenly discouraged my brothers and me from ever buying what we could not afford. So it was with much trepidation that in 1978, when I left university, I applied for my first mortgage to share ownership of a small house costing £6,500.

The social climate has significantly changed since then. With the move from student grants to loans over a decade ago, young people may leave college and enter the workplace with a debt up to five times my 1970s' mortgage, a debt endorsed by the higher education policies of successive governments. The culture they have inherited is not one of financial prudence and cautious spending, but one of easy credit and unbridled consumption.

And if you have a generation enabled to be cavalier in their borrowing, you encourage banks to be prodigious in their lending, and property agents to be unconstrained in setting house prices. And all of this is encouraged by interminable credit card mailings which promise to turn each pauper into a prince or princess.

'The wise man built his house upon the rock.' That line alludes to one of Jesus' parables about what you put your faith in, what holds you should all else collapse.

Jesus was not for a moment suggesting that faith in God was a security against financial ruin. That would have been naive in the extreme. What he was encouraging was a world view in which human happiness is not determined by the fluidity of the market, but by a commitment to the selfless and liberating values of the kingdom of heaven. Being generous is a much more transformative activity than securing yet another loan.

It seems to me that to subscribe to a culture of debt is not just to become vulnerable to unremitting avarice, it's also to put your faith in sinking sands. Keeping up with the Joneses is one thing, but being in bondage to credit companies is quite another.

20 September 07

power

Why did the dinosaur die?

Why did the dinosaur die?

I've been musing on that question over the past five weeks while working in North America, but not because I was on any archaeological dig.

I was in the USA when the nation groaned as the Canadian dollar outvalued its southern counterpart. I heard people talk about the economy (and particularly the national debt) in less than positive terms. I read that President Bush's ratings had fallen to an all-time low, with only 31% of the population believing that he was doing a good job.

I never heard anyone in Republican or Democrat constituencies express enthusiasm for the way things are going in Iraq. But I did see newspaper articles featuring battle-weary troops being told that substantial down time with their spouses was not an immediate option.

And yet in these same weeks, the White House called on other nations to help end the repressive regime in Cuba, and from the President, Vice President and Secretary of State came a variety of differently intoned hints about the possibility of action against Iran if it proceeded to develop nuclear capability.

So I began to ask, 'Why did the dinosaur die?'

Then I remembered the answer given in the book *Tomorrow's Child* by the Brazilian theologian Rubem Alves. 'The dinosaurs,' he wrote, 'disappeared not because they were too weak but because they were too strong.' A similar conclusion might be deduced from the story of David and Goliath where the giant who terrorised an opposition army found his demise because all his boasted strength failed to protect him from a small boy with a sling.

Now I don't believe for a moment that all the USA does is wrong. But I do wonder how much longer its favoured title of 'the world's only superpower' can encourage the presumption that it has the right to tell all lesser peoples how they should conduct their affairs.

I'm as reticent to encourage nuclear capability in Iran as anyone else, but I don't believe that the resolution lies in the superpower setting conditions for dialogue. How, for example, would the USA react if politicians in the regularly vilified Cuba said, 'We will negotiate with you if you first stop your sanctions and campaigns of misinformation.'

I suppose what convinces me of the need for a measure of accommodation in international affairs is my late-in-life realisation that in Jesus, God forsakes omnipotence to enter into dialogue with the people of earth. He never espouses the belief that those of a different culture or religion are to be dominated or suspected. Rather, in what was frustrating even to his disciples, Jesus sees in those who are different from himself a potential worth encouraging.

And I wonder what it would be like if, in the world of global politics, those who would be combatants identified the potential in each other rather than concentrated on the problem.

29 October 2007

people-trafficking

The new slavery

Until Saturday, I never knew how many brothels there were in Cambridge. I had to go to Salisbury to find out. And I wish I had taken with me the Glasgow taxi driver who complained last week about how too much taxpayers' money goes to finance foreigners.

But let me unpack a little.

I was at Sarum College ... attending one of many conferences held throughout Britain this year to commemorate the parliamentary bill passed 200 years ago which tolled the death knell for slavery in the British Empire.

While the transatlantic slave-trade may have been abolished a long time ago, other forms of inhumane coercion still exist. And two speakers at the conference addressed the specific issue of the multibillion-dollar industry of global trafficking in which women's bodies are bought and sold as if they were commodities like tea or sugar.

Tim Brain, the Chief Constable of Gloucestershire, indicated that Britain is an active player in this travesty whereby overseas women are duped into believing that the trip to the UK, for which they have scrimped and saved, will result in a place in higher education or a good job. Then they end up in a brothel.

These are not street-walkers touting for trade. These are women from Africa, Asia and Eastern Europe, who like 19th-century slaves, are confined to quarters where they do not know night from day.

Nor are they held captive in Soho, but in respectable neighbourhoods in cities like Cambridge, Peterborough and Sheffield where so-called 'personal services' advertised in local newspapers are the euphemism for sex-slavery.

In an operation across the British Isles last year, police visited 515 premises, and rescued 188 women of whom almost half had been the victims of trafficking from abroad.

Few people would be quick to identify a close similarity between the police and Jesus, the more so since he was harassed and arrested by the constables of his day. But I couldn't help remembering the story in the Gospels about how he was confronted with a crowd of men who brought a woman allegedly caught in the very act of adultery.

They wanted him to authorise stoning her to death. And he, knowing that was the legal penalty, invited whomever of them was guilt-free to throw the first stone. They all disappeared, the oldest first.

What's the comparison with the police? Well, they don't treat trafficked women as criminals, but rather see them as victims of a contemporary form of slavery organised by well-heeled men who probably, like my Glasgow taxi driver, despise foreigners for allegedly being subsidised by British taxpayers.

There is little proof to substantiate the taxi driver's opinion. But there is convincing evidence that whenever a British man uses a brothel, the chances are that he is subsidising slavery.

5th November 2007

St Andrew's Day

God's favourite colour

This being St Andrew's day, and I being in Newcastle, it is unlikely that I'll see glasses raised and hear, in my native tongue, the words:

> 'Here's tae us! Wha's lyke us?
> Damn few an they're a' deid!'

... which being translated means: 'Cheers! The only people we can emulate are deceased.'

That toast typifies an inferiority complex which at one time ran like a genetic fault line through many Scots.

I remember witnessing a classic exhibition of the disorder when travelling one night ages ago on the top deck of a no. 38 bus along Shaftesbury Avenue in London. Up stood an evidently inebriated Glaswegian and regaled the top deck with a litany of questions:

> 'Who gave ye yer penicillin? A Scotsman.
> An who gave ye yer television? A Scotsman.
> An who gave ye yer telephone? A Scotsman.'

This inquisition was terminated when a cockney voice from the back of the bus added to the litany by asking, 'And who gave you your whisky?'

Now, thank God, it is not simply dead heroes we extol.

On Monday I was again on a no. 38 bus, this time to go to

Sadler's Wells Theatre to see a new opera by James MacMillan. He, who lives in Glasgow, is one of the most profound and prolific composers of our day, and his opera *The Sacrifice* is a hallmark work.

Just a few days previously I had been in Vancouver where I heard a Canadian lecturer speak warmly of how two of the most significant contemporary English language novelists are Ian Rankin and Alexander McCall Smith, both of whom live in Edinburgh.

I suppose I could also allude to the number of cabinet ministers who are Scots or even muse on Dolly the sheep ... But I don't want to emulate the battle honours of my drunken compatriot on the no. 38 bus.

Sufficient perhaps to say that on our patron saint's day Scotland has more to celebrate than dead poets, bagpipes and golf.

But what about St Andrew ... who cannot claim European – never mind Scottish – pedigree? His connection to the country is tenuous and his profile in the Bible is not very high. If one were to give him a job description it would be that he introduces people to that which is greater than themselves. He did this with his brother Peter, with an adolescent boy and with Greek tourists. He brought them all to Jesus.

There's something both attractive and self-effacing about that, something genuinely humble about a life which introduces others to that which is greater than themselves. I hope my nation, in emulating St Andrew, can still do that ... as well as reminding the world that God's favourite colour is tartan.

30th November 2007

honesty

Trouble in telling the truth

Three years ago, I met a woman in British Columbia who had an unusual but by no means unique story.

She had been adopted at birth and raised very happily in a loving family. She married, had children of her own and was very secure in herself.

When she was in her late thirties, and for reasons of curiosity rather than psychological need, she thought she would try to trace her birth mother. Contact was made through a Canadian government agency. Conversations on the telephone eventually led to the woman meeting both her birth mother and father and eventually four brothers she never knew existed.

I remembered this when I read yesterday of the two Czech baby girls who had been born eighteen minutes apart and mistakenly given to each other's parents. This fact only came to light when the children were almost a year old. Given that each was being lovingly reared, was it right to breach happy family life and potentially confuse the babies by returning them to their natural parents?

One might say that it would take the wisdom of Solomon to discern what was appropriate. Happily we have recourse to that very wisdom, for when he, as king of Israel, was confronted with two women each of whom laid claim to the same baby, Solomon ordered the disputed child to be cut in two with a sword. On hearing his judgement, one of the women protested and said that her adversary should be given the child. Solomon did the very opposite. He awarded the child to the protester. Why? Because he perceived that the true mother was the one who sought the child's welfare, not her own.

As regards my friend in Canada, she had never known the identity of her birth mother nor did the birth mother know by whom her child had been adopted. But in the case of the Czech families, the truth of their identities and of the hospital's mistake was out. It had to be acted on. And though psychologists sensitively monitored the transition, both couples indicated that handing over their presumed daughter to her rightful parents was a painful process. The terrible mix-up caused them anguish as well as anger.

Indeed at one point one of the mothers said, 'She's my daughter. I cannot look at her in any other way. I cannot imagine separating from her.'

But how good it is for them that they decided to go through the inevitable pain rather than live with a troubling secret. And good also for their children. For how would these girls feel if twenty years from now either of them discovered that they had been the victim of deception by parents who hid the truth rather than shared it?

6th December 2007

carbon footprint

Unpaid wages

Wayne was shocked to discover on his arrival home that all the windows were open and the air conditioning was switched off.

… This may seem like the opening sentence in a trashy novel, but it's actually what happened a few years ago when I was staying with friends in the USA. They leave for work at eight and don't return until six in the evening. It being a hot day, I switched off the air conditioning and opened the windows. There was a slight hint of annoyance in Wayne's voice when he noted this change in domestic policy, so I asked him why he didn't put his air conditioning on a timer. He replied, 'Because I can afford it.'

The frustration articulated at the Bali summit over America's reluctance to sign the Kyoto Accord is understandable. Why should developing nations curb their greenhouse gas emissions if the world's major polluter refuses to do so? But for many decent Americans the fact that their standard of living enables them to afford what they want obliterates their need to be concerned.

This is not a peculiar transatlantic phenomenon. Many British citizens fly to mainland Europe for a weekend because endless adverts offering cheap air-fares make it more affordable to visit Prague than Edinburgh. Most of us, myself included, could compare the size of our wardrobe today with that of ten years ago and find we have an excess of clothes we barely wear for the simple reason that today clothes are relatively cheaper. We can afford them.

Yes, so we can. But can the world afford not just our affluence but also our presumption that what we can pay for, we should therefore have?

Christianity has not been so clear in its discussion of excessive consumption as the Jewish prophets were. One reason is that many Christians presume that Jesus came to supersede the prophets, whereas he came to endorse them. Another presumption is that the New Testament doesn't seem to address the issue explicitly.

But now and again, as in the book of James, we find words such as, 'The wages you have not paid the men who worked your fields cry out against you. And the cry of the reapers has reached the ears of the Lord of Hosts.'

This is pertinent to the Kyoto negotiations as western powers try to argue that nations like India and China should do more to cut pollution. The reason why their carbon footprint is so large is partly because they are wearing our old shoes.

Consumer goods for Britain and the USA are now invariably produced in Asia. For us to reduce global warming should require that we both curb our consumption and compensate other nations for the industrial effluent they produce on our behalf. These are the wages we have not paid. This is the compensation which is of interest to heaven.

13th December 2007

children

The abuses of affluence

For a very happy gap year in the '70s I worked in residential childcare, an experience which came flooding back to me the other day. It was triggered by the news from Jersey about allegations of abuse in a children's home.

Institutional abuse of young people is horrific. The psychological scars can cripple an individual's self-image for life, and destroy the possibility of close loving relationships. Perhaps that's why, in a rare allusion to children, Jesus said that anyone who forced a child to do wrong should be thrown into the sea with a millstone around his neck.

There is no excuse for child abuse. But there is a context which is seldom acknowledged.

When I was employed in childcare in the '70s, it was a job which few people wanted to do. The hours were long; you sometimes had to deal with aggressive behaviour; and, inevitably, you were the butt of jokes and name-calling. The pay was not very great; care staff were sometimes regarded as second-rate social workers, and there was no compulsory training. So, because there were not many takers for the jobs, it was possible for the wrong people to get a foot in the door.

Children's homes had a notoriously high turnover of staff, which could be disorienting to those in their care. A constantly changing cadre of staff members was able to go into the bedrooms of the kids, night and morning, and there was no talk of boundaries. This was just a generation ago, but there are some clear parallels with the workhouses of Dickens' day.

Now things are different. There is screening of employees, there are codes of practice which have to be agreed to, and children now have a vocabulary about their bodies which they did not have thirty years ago.

It is with hindsight that we see the flaws of the past and express amazement that people then were so short-sighted

But short-sightedness is not a phenomenon belonging solely to the past. So I want to ask: what will people say thirty years from now about the way we treat children today?

Will they applaud us for acquiescing to the phenomenon of pester-power, whereby parents cave in to the demands of their children for the most recent novelty being advertised as a must-have for adolescents? Will they extol a society where, in both rich and poor families, some mothers and fathers are afraid to say 'No'? Will they admire the way in which, to para-phrase Jesus, if a child asks for a conversation he is given a video game; or if she asks for a meal she is given a take-away to eat in front of the television?

Or will the recently published report from the Children's Society, which states that a majority of people interviewed believe that materialism actually harms children, be seen as a turning point?

Just as abuse in childhood can affect a person's whole life, so can indulgence. Children are gifts of God to be nurtured, not pets to be ignored or spoiled at our convenience.

27 February 2008

alcohol and community

In search of the diligent drinker

The Oban Times, like many conscientious local newspapers, offers the kind of information which seems to escape the notice of the national dailies ... such as the names of individuals who, worsened by drink, have been discovered urinating in public places.

It is unlikely, however, that this kind of naming and shaming will become a major plank in the government's attempt to deal with binge drinking. That thrives in an atmosphere of anonymity. People who commute from the suburbs to the city centre for a night on the tiles seldom have any connection to the place where they will exercise their freedom to drink as much as they want.

This cavalier behaviour is not as evident on the continent whose drinking culture we are so keen to emulate. But then, in a city like Amsterdam, there are few mega pubs. In the Rembrandt Square people sit in terraces, are served by waiters, casually watch passers-by, and engage in light-hearted banter – a far cry from the experience of being squeezed into a pressurised drinking-trough where the level of noise discourages conversation.

Nor is the behaviour so evident in Australia. Sydney, for example, has pubs where licensees employ someone to inform those who look the worse for wear that they have had their last drink. This proactive measure ensures a pleasant environment, and prevents licensees from being prosecuted for any antisocial behaviour caused in the streets by their customers.

In both these countries it is as if those involved in the

licensing trade had been given a seminar by St Paul, a man not averse to a drink himself. For, in writing about responsible behaviour, he makes the interesting comment:

'We are free to do anything?
Yes. But not everything is good for us.
We are free to do anything,
but not everything builds community.'

That's the missing dimension in Britain. What in the world of leisure builds up community?

The measures announced by the government to curb wrongful sales and hold licensees more accountable are to be welcomed. But to increase fines for disorderly behaviour and expect the police to continually face up to people who are too inebriate to speak intelligibly is primarily *post factum*. Perhaps we need something more radical.

What is required is for the places where people gather to be humanised, and for the relationship between staff and customers to be more than a financial transaction. And customers should know that, wherever you choose to drink, there is an obligation to behave responsibly, otherwise you will be asked to leave before the next drink makes you insensible.

Of course, this will not go down well with the brewers who will want to defend their freedom to earn as much as they can. But the freedom to consume drink and the freedom to sell it have to be seen in the overall context of what builds up rather than destroys community.

I have a friend who enjoyed going out so much that he was frequently called a drunkard and a glutton. I'm sure he would agree with this. He has four Gospels written about him.

4th March 2008

children

Like a child

There is little that connects the rural village of Lennoxtown near Glasgow with the seaside town of Buckhaven in Fife apart from shock and disbelief.

They stem from both being places where, last Saturday, children were murdered.

In Lennoxtown it was brothers aged six and two; in Buckhaven it was a seven-year-old boy and his older sister who had learning difficulties. And with cruel irony these brutal crimes took place on the anniversary of the still-mysterious abduction of the three-year-old Madeleine McCann.

We are horrified by the death or disappearance of children in a much more compelling way than should a similar fate befall an adult.

There is something about children ...

There *is* something about children, which is perhaps why Jesus, in looking for a model for membership of the kingdom of God, pointed to a child in the middle of a group of adults. 'Unless you become like this wee one,' he said, 'you'll never get in.'

What was he pointing to? The usual answer is innocence. But I totally discount that. I have been in too many houses where there are young children to regard innocence as their primary attribute.

But there is certainly a sense that children have been untouched by the world … their responses are more spontaneous than calculated. If I phone a colleague and his wife answers, she might say, 'My husband's not available at the moment.' But if I get his five-year-old daughter, she would be more liable to say, 'My daddy's in the toilet and he takes such a long time.'

That unaffected honesty, combined with wide-eyed trust, playfulness, a vivid imagination and a belief that tomorrow can be better than yesterday: all these virtues combine in children. And they're valued so highly by God that Jesus says that death by drowning would be a preferable fate to that which will befall those who pervert the natural development of children.

These words are uncompromising. They were intended for all time to protect the most vulnerable. But they were not spoken in judgement to a courtroom full of criminals. They were said to a group of responsible adults who probably thought that they would never harm a child.

Maybe Jesus was expressing in his way the wisdom enshrined in all faiths. Namely that if we do not live in love and awe of that which is much greater than ourselves, we may become tempted to damage or defile that which is much weaker.

6th May 2008

political healing

Recovery – the Western way

Imagine what it would be like if the Netherlands were swamped by a tidal wave, and you were marooned in your native village of Monnickendam. After a week, you see strangers in your garden. They come from a country which has called your leaders paranoid. They don't speak Dutch, and they offer you food you don't recognise.

Now think of Burma. I'm not an apologist for the cabal of generals who rule Myanmar. And certainly, if the accusations are true that they would rather have seen people die than be the recipients of aid, they must be guilty of wilful genocide. But should we be surprised if the leaders of a country which Western governments have accorded pariah status are reticent to defer to our wishes?

Myanmar cannot be compared to China just as it cannot be compared to Britain. It has two thirds of our population but three times the landmass. It has one major and eight minority languages. Almost 90% of the population are Buddhist and most live in rural areas. It has had ten days to deal with the devastation of a cyclone after more than ten years of sanctions imposed on the military elite by the very people who now want to be the saviours of its ordinary citizens.

With hindsight we realise that one of the mistakes in the occupation of Iraq was that few in charge seemed to understand either the underlying ethnic tensions, the Arab political mind or Middle-Eastern culture. And so we imposed on that country a constitution written by outsiders ... for whose benefit?

41

Such cultural ignorance may explain why the Burmese generals, even if they do not speak for the majority of citizens, are more reticent about welcoming unknown Western experts than they are about receiving the aid supplies now trickling into the country.

As I say, I could never condone a regime which is prepared to let people die. But I think that as willing benefactors we always need to ask ourselves: What will achieve the most effective response in this situation?

I say this because, as a Christian, I am constantly fascinated by the untidy way in which Jesus responds to need. His healing miracles occupy a fair proportion of the Gospels, but they have no common pattern.

In one place he heals in public, in another he heals in private and urges no publicity. In one instance he touches, in another he spits, in another he shouts. And when his disciples come to him confused with a case which hasn't responded to their ministrations, he gives them a row for not appreciating that something different from proven technique is required.

Suffering whether in the body or the body politic is always a mystery. Technical help may relieve pain, but it may require something beyond our trusted yet presumptuous instincts to bring complete healing.

13th May 2008

imperfection

Designer faults

I had Jed staying at my house last night. It was easier than the last time, much easier. In fact the last time he came to stay, I was on the point of cancelling his visit two days before his arrival. I had convinced myself that it wouldn't work.

He, Jed, must sound either like a dysfunctional nephew or a neighbour's maladjusted dog. But he's neither.

He's just a young man who happens to be blind, and always has been.

But having him in my house became a worry before his first visit. I persuaded myself that the house was too oddly shaped, too crowded with junk, that the staircase was too narrow, that he'd hit his head on one of the door lintels. I was on the verge of making an excuse and calling it off when I realised that the problem was not with him, but with me.

He had lived with blindness all his life but I had never had a blind person stay in my house. It was not his disability that was the issue, it was mine.

This was clear when after dinner he volunteered to wash the dishes. In my keenness to avoid any breakages, I forgot that he washed up every day in his own house. When I was apprehensive about his going out for a walk, I forgot that he did that every day and often in unfamiliar neighbourhoods. He wasn't the one who was limited; I was.

I intentionally reflect on this on the day after a contentious parliamentary debate on medical research issues, because I would hate us to delude ourselves into believing that one day science will or should eradicate all disorders, so that we can all be 'normal'.

The truth is that just as there are fault lines in the geology of the earth which cause earthquakes, there are fault lines in our DNA. There are fault lines in our physiology, there are fault lines in our psychology which are part of the given. God did not give us a perfect earth: God gave us a good earth. God did not give us perfect bodies: God gave us sufficient bodies. God did not give us perfect understanding: God gave us curiosity which is at the centre of all science.

And human fulfilment is not found in the creation of a hermetically sealed zone in which there is no one affected by limitation, disfigurement, psychosis or disease. Human fulfilment, at least as understood by Jesus, has more to do with the blind teaching the sighted how to be perceptive, the paralysed helping the agile to move carefully, those with Down's syndrome teaching those without it how to smile.

Maybe that's why Jesus told a man whose schizophrenia he had healed that he should stay in his community rather than leave it; and why to priests who knew how to pronounce people unclean, he sent back those whom they had rejected for complete reintegration.

20th May 2008

women

Women leading the way

In the wake of the Church of England's decision to proceed with the consecration of women as bishops, there has been both pain and rejoicing. The jubilant have predictably commented that this shows how the Church is catching up with society. That may be the case, but I don't think it has yet caught up with Jesus.

Let me explain ... or rather let me allude to a conference at which I was recently working in Canada. I divided participants into two groups. The first was asked to name Jesus' twelve male disciples and state three things we knew about each. The other was asked to identify twelve women who followed Jesus and state three things we knew about them ... all from memory.

I'd never done this before so I was as surprised at the outcome as anyone else.

None of those looking at the male disciples could remember any more than eight. Names like Nathaniel, Thaddeus and Simon the Zealot were not quoted. Of those identified, most people could only remember three things about Peter, John, Andrew and Judas. Yet, with the exception of Judas, the other eleven are men after whom churches throughout the world are named.

The group looking at the female disciples had no difficulty in identifying twelve women and were able to remember three things about the majority of them ... and not because they were 'fallen'.

Most surprising of all, we discovered that the woman whom Jesus met at a well is the only person in the four Gospels to whom a whole chapter is devoted. She's the first evangelist. Andrew brings his brother, a young boy and some Greeks to Jesus, for which he is made patron saint of Scotland. The woman at the well brings a whole village to Jesus, but no nation has so honoured her.

If you look further you see that it's women who give Jesus his declared models of faith, love and generosity. It's women who regularly provide food and lodgings for him and his male companions. It is the women who followed him, who accompany his body to the grave; and a woman who first sees him after the resurrection.

Is there another male figure in world history who has so clearly engaged with, depended on and encouraged women without the familiar accompaniments of seduction or exploitation?

Has there been a major Western politician who has been so explicitly trusting? A captain of British industry who has been so reliant? A top-ranking male academic who has been so collegial with women?

I suggest that the consecrating of female bishops is not the major issue. For both liberals and traditionalists the bigger issue is the feminisation of communities of faith until they are as representative and nurturing of the giftedness of women as Jesus was.

Now, if churches became like that they wouldn't be catching up with society, they would be leading it.

9th July 2008

sexuality

The love that dare not …

'Night after night on my bed, I have sought my true love.'

… This is not so much a personal testimony as a quotation from the Bible. It came to mind a few years ago when I was visiting a church in New Zealand where the congregation was exercised because a sex shop had opened up across the street. It had a large notice board which advertised items you wouldn't normally find at a Tupperware Party.

In discussing this predicament with the minister, I suggested that, since the church also had a large notice board, it might offer alternative inducements. Hence I proposed he might put up a poster saying,

> NIGHT AFTER NIGHT ON MY BED,
> I HAVE SOUGHT MY TRUE LOVE.
> WANT TO FIND OUT MORE?
> COME TO ST JOHN'S AT 6.30 ON SUNDAY.

The Song of Songs, from which that quotation comes, is not a book frequently read, although it says a lot about healthy erotic sex. It is attributed to King Solomon, who certainly knew quite a bit about the subject, having entertained 700 wives and 300 concubines. Curiously, though a direct ancestor of Jesus, he is never taken as a model of good practice.

Nor is Isaac … the son of Abraham and one of a number of biblical patriarchs with unusual dating practices. It is his father who sends a servant to find a wife for the boy. Subsequently, the servant brings back a girl called Rebecca to meet a man whom she has never seen. No sooner has Isaac met her than he takes her into his tent and beds her in consolation for the death of his mother.

I don't think I've been at a wedding ceremony yet where the vicar asks the groom, 'Do you come here earnestly seeking marriage to this woman because you are missing your mum?'

Nor, come to think of it, have I ever heard a minister ask a couple, 'Do you come here seeking holy matrimony because that is preferable to burning with desire?' ... yet that perspective on marriage is offered by St Paul.

It is interesting how, in matters of human sexuality, Christians feel free to pick and choose the bits that suit them. We elevate to the status of a litmus test of piety one aspect of sexuality about which the Bible is comparatively silent. (I'm sure you'll know the issue to which I'm alluding without my having to be explicit.*) And yet more positive expressions we leave alone, like seeking my true love on my bed night after night.

... Ditto for the Ethiopian eunuch. He never gets much of a mention in hymns, prayers or preaching. Is it perhaps because only Scots can easily pronounce his 'condition'? At any rate, he is the first adult whose baptism is explicitly recorded in the New Testament. Even though as a eunuch he would have been spurned and victimised by some communities because of his 'irregular sexuality', he was embraced and totally accepted by the fragile fledgling church.

I wonder if that story has any bearing on the current divisive issue, the name of which I will not mention.

18th July 2008

* At the time of publication ministers of the Church of Scotland, of which the author is one, have been forbidden to speak publicly about homosexuality until a Special Commission set up by the Church's General Assembly has had its findings discussed.

health

The care of welfare and wellness

I wonder what Hamish McKechnie would say if, on visiting the health clinic to see about changing his medication for angina, the doctor were to remark,

> 'Well, Mr McKechnie. You're 18 stone. You're carrying too much weight and you're still smoking. So come back in 3 months when you've lost 20 lbs and cut down on the cigarettes, and then we'll discuss your medication.'

Or what would Shirley Adamson say if, at a parents' evening in the local primary school, she asked her son's teacher what was being done to do tackle the boy's attention deficit syndrome, and the teacher replied:

> 'Mrs Adamson, if you remove the mobile phone, iPod and television from your son's bedroom every night by 11 o'clock, and if you stop feeding him sugary food and fizzy drinks for breakfast, then I might be willing to talk about his education.'

I imagine that if these replies were given to Mr McKechnie and Mrs Adamson (both fictional characters of course), they would possibly report the doctor and the teacher either to a local health or education monitoring agency or to their appropriate professional association.

And they would make a fuss. Because there are standards, league tables, independent inspections which are supposed to guarantee success. And this week, in the case of General Practitioners, scrutiny of their work seems set to become tighter.

Putting the screws on health and education professionals is a popular ploy of politicians of all parties. After all, our taxes pay for these people, and we expect results!

But apart from being legalistic, that attitude suggests that we, the consumers of health and education services, can somehow exonerate ourselves from responsibility for our own welfare and that of our progeny.

In the New Testament, particularly through the forensic mind of St Paul, we see that within us all there is a constant tension between legalism and grace. Legalism is an attitude which believes that regulations and measurable results are what win the day. But grace is a much more arbitrary thing. It comes not from external decree, but from internal generosity of spirit, from kindness, sensitivity and love. It's seen in Jesus who prefers to invite people into a personal relationship rather than to publish a failsafe list of dos and don'ts for successful living.

And for the good of our health and education services, I suggest that grace is required of us, as co-partners with professionals in caring for our bodies and our children.

After all, what really can medicine or education do to a body or to child if either is denied that fond yet thoughtful cherishing on which all life thrives?

25th July 2008

Barack Obama

The need for a new world order

I've just come back from three weeks in the USA, working in very different places ... among rampant liberals in Arizona (for which state John McCain is senator), and at the cream of conservative evangelical colleges in Illinois (for which state Barack Obama is senator).

In these and other places I visited, people expressed surprise that the British should be so knowledgeable about American politics. Some, indeed, were slightly dismayed when I said that people in countries outside the USA felt disenfranchised regarding the forthcoming election. After all, if the world's most powerful leader was about to be elected, should the rest of the world not be given some say as to who that might be? Having just come through a global financial crisis in which America sneezed and the rest of the world caught the flu, we surely deserve someone in the White House who has an international perspective.

This will certainly be evident in Barack Obama. It's not just that within his genes he combines both sides of the Atlantic, and has an awareness of two major faith traditions. Nor is it just because (unlike the majority of his compatriots) he has a passport and has travelled outside North America.

It's also because he was reared in a state which used to be a sovereign nation. For Hawaii was an independent Pacific kingdom until, at the end of the 19th century, the sons and daughters of Protestant missionaries encouraged the USA to invade the Pacific archipelago. Having no army, Hawaii was quickly taken, the queen was imprisoned, and the country was ruled from Washington without ever a plebiscite of the inhabitants.

For those who know this episode of American history, as Obama does, it is a constant reminder of how the maxim 'Might is Right' is often assumed by nations which believe that they have a divine mandate. The USA – like Spain in South America, Holland in South Africa and Britain which allegedly rose first from the azure main 'by heaven's command' – has a history of believing that its nation's imperialism was ordained by God.

Those days, certainly as regards the USA, are surely now over. No nation, no matter how many people attend worship, or what statement of faith appears on its currency, has a divine right to dominate another. So, under this new presidency there will need to be a curtailing of suspicion and condemnation of those countries which, for good reason, have chosen not to subscribe to the American dream.

Obama is a Christian. He therefore follows a man who at his birth possibly received gifts from Iraqis, during his life enjoyed the company of Syrians and en route to the cross was helped by a Libyan. Let's hope that the axis of evil may be superseded by a tenure of grace.

5th November 2008

money

A primary moral issue

One of the great privileges of my life is being able to travel and work in countries outside the United Kingdom. That such an experience broadens the mind was clear to me when, in the '70s, I worked in the Netherlands and there was able both to realise that the politics of Britain were not the only politics, and to gain a more objective understanding of my native land.

I sometimes wish such a perspective were possible for the inhabitants of the USA which, of all Western nations, must have the smallest percentage of its inhabitants in possession of a passport. Hence some Americans tend to think that their priorities and opinions are the only ones that matter.

In my recent conversations with both Democrats and Republicans in the States, there was an element of surprise when I indicated that people of faith in other parts of the world did not espouse America's perspective on burning moral issues.

At a meeting, someone asked what I thought about the 'culture wars'. I presumed this referred to differences in aesthetic taste whereby some Christians believe that no good music was written after Bach died, while others believe that only the latest offering from glamorous religious pop stars is good enough for God.

But that was not the issue. The 'culture wars' question had to do with how people take diametric positions on the unholy trinity of abortion, stem-cell research and same-sex relationships. Thus morality is defined in terms of what affects the bodies of individuals rather than the body politic.

Although it may seem offensive to some, I think that an exclusive obsession with these issues is, to use a phrase of Jesus', like 'choking on a fly while gulping down a camel'. My American hosts were not best pleased when I suggested that the biggest moral issue which the USA and the West had to face is what we do with money.

For, never mind the yet-to-be-conceived child, if western governments do not fulfil their promise to free Africa from debt by 2010, then it will be the born child who will die. If in the USA there continues to be a nationwide disparity in funding basic health care, then – never mind stem-cell research – people currently being made homeless and jobless will live in fear of becoming ill.

The next four years will, for the good of the world, require that the new president looks on money as a primary moral issue.

For it is a moral issue to go back on promises of refinancing the global south. It is a moral issue to import manufactured goods at a price that ensures the producers earn less than subsistence wages. It is a moral issue to reprimand people who cheat on social security claims, while showing indifference to millionaires who are rewarded even when they cause financial calamity.

Wouldn't it be great if America gave a lead on these moral issues?

5th November 2008

prophecy

Voices from the edge

There is a phrase which I heard twice on the *Today* programme on Friday and read several times in the newspapers over the weekend. It has almost become a mantra when something has gone wrong in the economy, in politics, or in welfare, educational or health services. It is the phrase 'Lessons will be learned'.

I would gladly censor that convenient aphorism. It is lazy news-speak, diplomatic flannel, a multi-purpose euphemism. In nearly every case what the speaker means to say is:

'I can't believe our failsafe system has imploded.'
Or: 'I don't know who's to blame yet, but heads will roll.'

It inevitably leads to a committee of enquiry being set up to scrutinise and make recommendations. It is always *post factum*, after the event. And it nearly always happens in situations where the prophetic voice has been ignored.

In the season of Advent, we are encouraged to listen for such voices. They are not the meanderings of fortune tellers whose palms have been greased to flatter the customer. The prophet is someone who reads into the present state of society and discerns two things: the consequence of present actions in advance of a crisis, and an alternative reality which is worth striving for.

I suspect that if Isaiah were around today he would not be surprised at the disquiet surrounding social work departments.

Ten years ago he would have said to unsympathetic ears:

> 'If you burden social workers with case-loads they can't manage, and require them to spend as much time on paperwork as on client contact, and then use them and teachers as whipping boys when things go wrong, they will never give of their best.'

I suspect that if Amos were around today he wouldn't be surprised by the global financial crisis.

Ten years ago he would have said:

> 'If you encourage a culture of debt, put few restrictions on what people can borrow, allow unbridled consumerism to run wild, the economy will crash.'

If Jeremiah were around today, he wouldn't be surprised by the fragility of the planet caused by a cavalier approach to ecology. He would point to what he said two-and-a-half millennia ago:

> 'Your wrongdoing will upset nature's order, and your sins will terminate her generosity.'

Sometimes for good and honourable reasons, sometimes for reasons of political expediency, the prophetic voices are not given the hearing that they deserve as necessary correctives to the prevailing norms in politics as in faith. But it's at our own peril that we ignore them. For they remind us not just that prevention is better than cure, but also that insight is better than hindsight.

Prepared but not broadcast 8th December 2008

self-delusion

The danger of religion in politics

As a believer, I would never vote for a political party which claimed to be Christian.

I would never do that because history bears witness to countless regimes which believed they were God's answer to a nation's prayers. And with that smug arrogance which is sometimes a by-product of religiosity, crusades have been launched, Jews have been exterminated, Africans have been enslaved, and theological doctrines like apartheid have found political expression, favouring the powerful and subjugating the poor.

Nor would I vote for an MP solely on the ground that he or she was a person of faith. I don't ask my doctor if she is Muslim or a practising Catholic before entrusting myself to her. What essentially concerns me is whether she is good at her chosen profession. Being a born-again Christian or a devoted Sikh is no guarantee of excellence in matters of medical diagnosis or parliamentary debate.

At the same time, it is a sad reflection on the British nation if people of faith entering politics feel obliged to play down the importance of religion in their lives. I am referring, of course, to the sentiments expressed by our former prime minister Tony Blair, who recently indicated that he felt his credibility would have been compromised had he been more open about his beliefs.

If a Member of Parliament were to reveal on *Desert Island*

Discs that his or her primary musical diet was maudlin Country and Western, no one would fear for a lack of clarity in political judgement. But to admit a belief in God is to risk becoming an object of derision in a way that would be deemed reprehensible in many other countries.

The decisions which politicians make are never rooted in neutrality. They will be coloured by a variety of experience. Working abroad, being brought up on an island, being black, gay, orphaned as a child or made redundant as an adult ... all these will influence choices as much as any party manifesto. And religious faith should have a similar benign potential.

In the first instance, all world religions have perspectives on the value of the earth we inhabit and the people who surround us. These perspectives provide a corrective to the self-interest and egocentricity that might otherwise dominate decisions.

Secondly, if religious faith enables people to sustain their commitment to public life, and provides nourishment for their spirit, what is there to fear?

What people might fear is an apprehension I share, namely that any politician can develop a saviour syndrome, and either take decisions without reference to political colleagues or make religious pronouncements without the assent of his or her faith community.

That's where it's important to have a good atheist psychiatrist at hand, not to correct a religious problem, but to deal with self-delusion.

15th December 2008

consumption

The cost of cheapness

I don't know why Piebald Lindsay was so called. It might have been because his head was as hairless as a goldfish bowl. Or it might have been because of his pony. But at any rate, he was a lousy trumpet player.

That was the first sound you heard when his horse and cart entered our street in the '60s. Then came the shout, 'Toys for rags! Money for rags!' That was the cue to pester our mothers for an old shirt or pullover to exchange for balloons or trinkets. But Piebald got fussy. When what were called 'man-made fibres' began to appear in clothing, he never accepted them. He wanted cotton or wool.

Nowadays, there are no ragmen. Instead we have 'nearly new shops'. Some people say they are a sign of poverty. Actually they are an index of wealth. They indicate how, as distinct from the '60s when mothers made shirts and knitted jerseys, today we can purchase such things at a comparatively lower price.

The reason, of course, is that most clothes are no longer made in Britain. They come from Asia .They cost less.

Oh, do they? Or is someone else or something else picking up the tabs?

A recent report identifies that while Britain claims to have lowered its carbon emissions by 18% since 1990 (thus fulfilling our obligations under the Kyoto Accord), China has increased its emissions by 15%. 'Good for Britain! Bad for China!' we might say. Not so. All that has happened is that industries which once threatened the climate here are now based elsewhere. If we were to own the amount of China's effluent produced for United Kingdom imports, our carbon emissions would be 20% higher not 18% lower. The environment is paying for our cheap clothing.

Cheapness always costs. That's an insight as old as God. Jesus says as much when he comments on how no one in their right mind would think of erecting a building or fighting a battle if they did not work out in advance whether they could finance the project or had a sufficient fighting-force. What seems like a cheap deal does not assure a quality product.

Piebald Lindsay knew that cheapness costs. The production of synthetic materials terminated his livelihood as a ragman dealing in natural fibres. The expanding British waistline bears visible witness to it: the rise in obesity is directly associated with diets of cheap food high in sugar and starch, low in nutrients. The proliferation of Happy Hour drinking illustrates the same maxim, as cut price alcohol exacts its cost in long-term threats to the nation's health.

But a bargain is so tempting.

Well, Lent starts today ... time to give up cheapness and take up quality.

25th February 2009

alcohol abuse

A question of consumption

When is enough enough?

It's a tricky question. For the answer depends on whether the individual concerned is male or female, pregnant, diabetic, a teetotaller, on prescribed medication, a child or a pensioner.

And the reply, 'I know when I've had enough,' is too subjective to be sufficient, especially if the respondent is a novice or an inebriate.

I'm talking about alcohol, a perennial issue in social life and politics to which the Scottish government is directing its attention. The possibility is that legislation may soon be introduced to restrict alcohol consumption by outlawing bar-gain-priced booze and by permitting local authorities to raise the minimum age for purchasing strong drink. This would not be a European first. After Sweden was nearly crippled by alcohol abuse at the end of the 19th century, its government put severe restrictions on consumption. Even today Swedish off-sales premises are state controlled.

The Scottish government has come in for severe criticism from the drinks industry and some libertarians who speak of a 'nanny state' limiting freedom of choice. The argument is that if we educate people correctly, they should be able to consume wisely.

This is a bit disingenuous. We teach children road safety, and require drivers to pass a test. But nobody says that speed bumps and motorway restrictions are signs of a nanny state.

A more pertinent objection would be that there is no guarantee that restricting the sale of alcohol diminishes its abuse. All that might happen is the production of more criminals. For, as no less an authority than St Paul pointed out, one of the direct effects of law-making is to increase the recorded incidence of law-breaking. Laws don't in themselves make for goodness. Alcohol abuse is a cultural phenomenon which, like sectarianism or racism, will not suddenly disappear because of legislation. Tricky, isn't it?

But another angle on the issue appears when we juxtapose personal freedom with social well-being. As the American theologian Rheinhold Niebuhr pointed out, if we move from considering the good of the individual to the good of the community, we must talk about justice, which he described as the 'political currency of love'.

So, is it *just* that families are impoverished and wives abused because a man exercises his right to spend the household income on cheap drink?

I have some sympathy with the view that when you legislate against every potential lapse, you diminish personal responsibility. But, for me, the freedom of individuals to jeopardise their health and other people's safety should not be put on a higher plane than the obligation of a government to promote the common good.

4 March 09

singing together

Cum cantibus in choro

It may not be long before the tabloids sport headlines such as *Mendelssohn on the Mersey* or *Rachmaninov in Raploch* ... and all because there are *More than Maracas in Caracas*.

Last week, the Simón Bolívar Orchestra from Venezuela performed in Britain. Its first concert earned a rare five-star rating in *The Guardian*. All the instrumentalists in this ensemble are under 24. And many come from backgrounds where classical music would not have been a life choice were it not for a project called El Sistema which, in 30 years, has tutored 400,000 children and set up 150 orchestras in what is still regarded as a 'developing nation'.

The scheme is now being introduced in Britain. It has already started in Scotland, in Raploch, a deprived neighbourhood on the outskirts of Stirling. The project there is called 'Big Noise'. Last week the chairman of the project commented, 'It costs about £2,000 per year for a child to be taught in the Big Noise; but if the child ends up in the criminal justice system, it costs £18,500 per year.

Does this mean that classical music is the antidote to criminality? No, that would be a naïve assertion. But I'm reminded of a comment made by the head teacher of a primary school I once visited in Yorkshire. Its 190-strong choir included every child who did not go home for lunch. The head had made class singing a priority, an essential feature of the curriculum, and commented that one result was a noticeable decrease in behavioural problems.

'Why so?' I asked her and she said, 'You can pay a fortune for sports equipment and instructors and one of the by-products is to make children competitive. You hire a part-time singing teacher and you make children cooperative.

Maybe this is why in Christian churches music has such a high priority ... not just the practised music of performers, but the sound of untutored voices doing something magnificent together.

For, of all the arts, music is the most participative. We cannot all paint or perform a play together, but we can all sing. And the Bible sees this cooperative activity not as an option, but as a response to a divine command, 'Sing me a new song ... ,' says God.

In a highly competitive society, there's something to be treasured in a pursuit which costs little apart from time.

Maybe this is what differentiates us from the beasts ... that we make music not to attract suitors or display skill, but because cooperation is what we need to learn in order to prevent our race from dying.

20th April 2009

use of money

Good money

I want to say a good word about money, because too many bad words are being said.

Money is just not good news at the moment for most people. For some the budget has been a disappointment; for others the issue of MPs' expenses is a scandal; and for yet others the continuation of bumper rewards to bankers who have over-seen financial failure is outrageous.

Money is not enjoying a positive profile.

Indeed it has accrued to itself a phalanx of adjectives which suggest that it is inherently corrupt:

Filthy lucre,
Black economy
Back-handers
Shady deals
Toxic loans.

What we fail to see is that the more we use such terms, the more we suggest that money is inherently contaminated. Therefore, when we are involved with it, we may subconsciously believe that we are dealing with something unhealthy. So we slip into being economical with the truth when we speak of financial matters. Married people refrain from telling their spouses how much they earn; close friends rarely discuss their personal wealth; and in the public realm deceit, silence or embarrassment surround the issues of expenses, taxation and the identity of those who are the gatekeepers of the black holes into which so much money seems recently to have disappeared.

Christians who refuse to be open about money, and who thereby encourage secrecy in high and low places, most need to be challenged. For the Christian tradition in its holy books never attributes a moral value to money, nor does it automatically dub wealthy people as duplicitous or malevolent.

Half of Jesus' parables mention money and never in condemnation. And when he upturns the tables of currency changers in the Temple, it is not coinage he is objecting to, but those who mishandle it.

It is ultimately our use of this commodity which has a beneficial or detrimental effect on other people. It is not pounds or dollars that are shady, it is how they are employed. It is not the economy that is deceitful, it is how banks, business, the government and taxpayers are transparent or furtive about their dealings.

The *trickle-down effect* was the process whereby the wealthy were encouraged to enhance their fortunes in the belief that financial amelioration would spread from the top down. The fact that it hasn't worked has nothing to do with a complex economic logjam. It has all to do with how benevolence, generosity and justice do not automatically flow from a huge income.

Money in itself is morally neutral. But its ability to benefit a society only becomes apparent when those who have it also have nothing to hide.

27th April 2009

poetry

Poet's pleasure

How could Wordsworth know what it was like to *wander lonely as a cloud that floats on high* before the advent of air travel?

Did a field-mouse actually hear Burns calling it a *wee sleekit, cowerin, tim'rous beastie*?

And what proof is there that *Britain **first** at heaven's command arose out of the azure main*?

Answers on a postcard would not be welcome, partly because these are rhetorical questions, and also because the quotations come not from the annals of history but from the treasury of British poetry.

Who knows, in years to come, verses and couplets from the new Poet Laureate, Carol Ann Duffy, may flow off the tongue as easily as lines from Shakespeare or Dylan Thomas.

And if they do, it will be because Carol Ann Duffy's poetry is particular. She said as much in a newspaper interview at the weekend: 'I will write what needs to be written: I wouldn't write a poem if it felt forced.'

A few years ago I heard a similar comment from Huub Oosterhuis, a Dutch Jesuit. When asked if he would write a poem about anything, if commissioned, he replied, 'If I am asked to write a text for a child's birth or baptism, I'll produce something because I know what it feels like to hold a baby. But if I am asked to celebrate in verse the assumption of the blessed

Virgin Mary into heaven, I will plead agnosticism.'

Oosterhuis, Carol Ann Duffy, Robert Burns and William Wordsworth will have their work and words remembered not because they aimed to please, but because they allowed their imaginations to be present to the stimulus of the present moment.

Sometimes in my work I am amazed at how, when people read the Psalms (which are essentially religious poems with a 2,500-year-old pedigree), men and women in the 21st century are sometimes moved by lines such as:

Keep all my tears stored in your flask.
or *Darkness is now my only companion.*
or *You have spread a table before me in the presence*
of my enemies.

These words come from a moment in the poet's life when, oblivious to public approval, he or she has been present to the joy or pain of life, the beauty or terror of the world, the presence or absence of God. And because the experience has been so particular, the inspired verses speak to and for people in similar situations generations later.

It's the antithesis of that annual orgy of populist taste commonly know as the Eurovision Song Contest, where writers all over the continent try to concoct catchy jingles intended to win votes. But a year later, who remembers the entries?

Good poetry shall stand time's test;
Verse meant to please leaves few impressed.

4th May 2009

music

In tune with heaven

If you were listening to this programme around this time yesterday, you might have heard the very distinctive sound of a ukulele. I wonder where that took you.

If you are a man or woman of a certain age, it might have been evocative of George Formby *leaning on a lamppost at the corner of the street.*

Or you may have heard that instrument playing a tune which transported you to the first time you heard the last movement of Beethoven's 9th symphony; or to a church where first you sang the words, 'Joyful, joyful, we adore you'. Or the tune might even have dumped you at the headquarters of the European Union in Brussels.

Music takes us into other places because it's a highly associative phenomenon. When I hear Cat Stevens singing *Morning Has Broken*, half of me goes to the village of Bunessan on the island of Mull where the tune was first transcribed, and the other half goes to Dalston Market in London where I bought the album *Teaser and the Firecat* for 75 pence in 1972.

So, it was a bit of a shock the other day to ask an 18-year-old what was his favourite song and hear no immediate reply. Instead he produced an MP3 player on which he had access to as many albums as he wanted, at any time of day he wanted, in any part of the world in which he might be located. But nothing in the music connected him to anything other than his own immediate state of mind. It was as if he were being robbed of his past.

69

I was stunned to silence. It seemed as if that great ability of music to associate us with time and place and other people, to enable our own history to be allied to sound … that great mystery which even Jesus knew … had vanished.

I say 'which even Jesus knew' because there is a moment in the Gospels where, after the priests object to his applauding the untutored voices of street children, to their horror he pulls out a line from an old song about how God loves to hear children singing.

The story of music is replete with moments when new sounds burned themselves into both personal and corporate memory: the sight of King George III rising to his feet in wonder at Handel's *Hallelujah Chorus*; the riot that took place when Stravinsky's *Rite of Spring* was premiered; the reawakening of hope for the victims of apartheid when one voice in a crowd would encourage others to sing *Nkosi Sikelel' iAfrika*.

Music is the art form closest to faith, because unlike literature or painting it does not take its substance from the known world. It comes – melody, harmony, rhythm – from the beyond. But it takes on flesh when, played or sung in our presence, it becomes allied to a particular place, time and company. It is not a consumerist commodity. It is a treasure buried in a field which, when cherished, can be an intimation of heaven.

12th June 2009

medical provision

Health under attack

There are certain words which, when spoken, will divide any company into the cognoscenti and the bemused. One such word is colonoscopy. Since I mentioned I was going to have one, I discovered that five friends had beaten me to it.

Those who haven't had one might imagine that a colonoscopy is an advanced course in English grammar. But it's not that kind of colon, as ensuing conversation at your breakfast table may elucidate.

At any rate, it didn't take long, was accompanied by good humour and followed by a nice cup of tea and a cheese sandwich. And there was no charge.

I feel as if I should have had the event filmed and sent to CNN News in the USA to illustrate how well a national health service can function.

For these words, National Health Service (much easier to remember than colonoscopy), divide the American nation into those who know what happens in the UK and those who are ignorant, but out of a fear of government power creeping into an area of personal choice, berate President Obama's healthcare reforms. One well publicised ploy of the objectors is to highlight the real or imagined defects of our NHS, as if the world's richest nation, in which one in six people cannot afford healthcare insurance, is defect-free.

For some Americans, the issue is primarily one of money.

Why should those who can afford to pay private health insurance subsidise a system for those who can't? For Britain, I believe the matter is more a spiritual issue: human beings deserve good care, irrespective of whether they are wealthy or poor, occasionally ill or congenitally disabled, physically unwell or socially inadequate.

If that doesn't sound too spiritual, let me put it another way. I could quote John Donne saying no man is an island, all are connected to the main. But instead I'll just note that Jesus continually touched and was touched by people who were ill. And he expected his followers to behave similarly. He demonstrated that our full humanity is dependent on our being affected by the pain as well as the joy of others. His miracles weren't so much magic cures as indications of how healing happens when pain and compassion affect each other.

There was a girl of 14 having a colonoscopy the day I had mine, and a man in his late seventies. There was a rough-spoken plumber and a very erudite dowager, all benefiting from a health service whose principles seem to be more in keeping with the kingdom of heaven than a scheme where the wealthy pay and the poor perish.

14th August 2009

entrusting

Vox humana

Two weeks ago I was in Vietnam. I had always wanted to go there ever since I protested against the Vietnam war in the early seventies.

I had no idea what to expect. I knew no one there, nor did I know anyone who had visited the country. I was aware that it was a communist state and that in the past century it had been at odds with the French, the Chinese, the Japanese and the Americans. Oh ... and someone told me that the Vietnamese ate monkey brains.

So it took me by surprise when, sitting in the park opposite my hotel, hardly an hour in the country, three boys all aged 22, but looking younger, came up and said, 'Can we speak with you?'

I said, 'You're already doing that.'
'In English?' they asked.
'I'll try hard,' I replied.

Then they explained how for them, as graduates, it was important to improve their language skills if they were going to get anywhere in their chosen fields of economics, geology and accountancy.

I said to them, 'Look, I've just arrived. But if you want to speak English, come back tomorrow night at the same time, same place, and I'll take you for a meal.' The next night they returned and we went to a totally authentic Vietnamese restaurant. It was far away from the tourist track where

Americans and Australians sipped Western beer while commenting on local culture.

We met again on two other evenings. And on the last occasion, late at night, when two of the boys had gone to buy street food, the third, called Phu'oc, said to me, 'Could you sing me a song from your country?'

So I sang a song my parents used to sing to each other, one that was sung at my mother's funeral, a love song by Robert Burns – *Ae Fond Kiss*. And then I said to Phu'oc, 'Will you sing me a song from your country?' And with a voice like that of an angel, he sang a song he had learned from his grandparents, a song celebrating the landscape of the Mekong Delta.

I was very moved. Indeed, of all that I encountered in that visit, this experience of being sung to touched me most deeply. And I realised that if I hadn't taken the risk of entrusting myself to people of a very different culture and – possibly – of no religious persuasion, I would have missed out on a moment I will treasure all my life.

I tell this story because apart from today being St Andrew's Day, when Scottish songs will be sung all over the world, it is also the beginning of the season of Advent ... a season which really has nothing to do with fairy lights or turkeys or little donkeys, or excess presents. It is about God taking the risk of entrusting himself to people who did not know him, of whom some would have no religious persuasion, so that *they* might touch *him*.

30 November 2009

what really matters

Is it worth it?

Years ago, when I was a youth worker, we used to play a game called The Value Auction. It involved everyone being given a certain amount of paper money which they could use to purchase commodities put up for sale.

The twist was that while some things like a Caribbean cruise or a season ticket for the football stadium of your choice were immediately attractive, others were less so.

How much, for example, would you bid for a long life, or a happy marriage? How much would you bid to be able to start a family, or care for a dependent relative? The material things were the easiest to deal with, but the relational things, the things that involved quality rather than quantity, were less easy to deliberate on.

Stupid game, some might say. But we are entering a pre-election period when something similar is happening as our political parties set out their stalls, hoping that what is offered will attract the highest number of bidders.

And a very disparate assortment of commodities will – as it were – come under the hammer: the defence budget, overseas development, levels of taxation, welfare services, initiatives to deal with climate change. Which package will we bid for?

… Or perhaps a better question would be: 'What are we entitled to?'

The phrase 'the transvaluation of values' is variously attributed to Nietzsche, the philosopher, and to Reinhold Niebuhr, the American theologian. It is an interesting concept, that time can transform or invalidate the importance once given to objects or qualities. For our purpose the 'transvaluation of values' might pertain to how what once were luxuries sometimes become gradually transformed into necessities. A culture of entitlement develops in which, egged on by commercial advertising and political promises, we are led to believe that we are missing so much that we really deserve.

It's like that moment in the Gospels where the devil says to Jesus, 'All this I will give you, if only you will worship me.' And Jesus says, 'No. I don't need all that' ... and goes on to begin a public ministry in which he makes it clear that being is more important than having, relating more important than possessing.

I would not for a minute want to suggest that our political parties are as devious as the devil. But they do offer allurements and we have to make judgements.

So I wonder ... Being rather than having; relating rather than possessing ... Are these perhaps yardsticks by which we may gauge whether what we are asked to bid for is of ultimate value?

20 January 2010

child abuse

Prevention is better than ...

Just a glance at the Pope's pastoral letter to the church in Ireland is enough to confirm that it is lengthy, inclusive and detailed ... an exceptional document as several commentators have indicated.

I think that if I were a priest in that church I'd go down on my knees before my congregation and ask for forgiveness ... and that not out of personal guilt. When an institution through its silence seems to condone child abuse, then all in leadership – including the innocent – must share responsibility.

Given the control which the Church in Ireland has long held over education, the degree of potential contact between aberrant priests and innocent children has been considerable. However, it would be wrong to think that child abuse was a phenomenon specific to religious establishments.

Years after I left employment in child care for a London borough, I returned to my previous workplace and enquired after former colleagues who had worked in other children's homes. I was astounded to discover that some of them, who had seemed the most decent of men, were serving time for abusing those in their care.

If child abuse is a phenomenon that won't go away, then it is right that those in close contact with children should be screened. But screening doesn't eradicate desire ... and it is the desire or temptation to abuse children that needs more attention. We have signs in public places telling people what to do if they suspect they have a propensity towards alcoholism. But what do you do if you suspect you are a paedophile?

At university in the seventies, I was elected president of the Students' Representative Council at a time when my university had no counselling service. One day a 20-year-old student came into my office and asked if he could speak to me. He first told me that he felt called by God to the priesthood. And then he said that he wanted to admit to a sexual attraction to children.

'Why are you telling me this?' I asked. 'Because,' he said, 'I can't keep this secret any longer. It's too dangerous. I need to tell somebody. And I need to promise somebody that I will never ever harm children.'

What would you have done? I never knew his name. Had he said he was a sex offender, my response would have been clear and straightforward. But this was different. He had somehow found the courage to admit to a potential he swore he would never pursue.

Punishment after the event is not enough. Children will have been hurt. Yet we can't castrate or criminalise people who admit that there is within themselves a tendency they never wanted to be born with.

Is it possible to affirm the potential for good that is in them, while holding them accountable for ensuring that they are the only ones who will ever deal with the demons inside?

22 March 2010

power v humility

Bows and arsenals

Prague is the only city in which I have seen an orchestra wearing gloves. It was minus two in the concert hall. When I came into the street outside, at one degree Celsius it seemed like a heat wave.

So, Prague was a very appropriate place in which yesterday Russia and America affirmed the end of the Cold War by reducing their nuclear stockpiles.

I trust that instead of clouds of frosted breath, there was a rainbow over the city. That would have been very appropriate. Though perhaps the symbolism is lost on those who associate the rainbow primarily with New Age spirituality or Gay Pride. The rainbow actually has a much older symbolic pedigree.

It goes back to one of these early stories in the Bible which have more to do with mystery than history ... the story of how God was so angry at the way human beings were conducting themselves that he decided to flood the world. Only a few people – Noah and his family, and a sampling of animals huddled in an ark – survived.

And when the waters went down, when God contemplated how much had been annihilated, he vowed never to destroy the earth again ... and as a sign he put a rainbow in the sky.

Now what exactly did the rainbow signify? The bow – then as now – was an armament ... God's weapon of mass destruction ... hung in the sky so that the whole earth could see that it had become redundant.

God vowed never again to destroy the earth. But humanity has been reticent to make such a pledge. Through decades in which much of the world has been hungry, thirsty, diseased or poor, we have increased the size of dangerous and expensive arsenals. As regards nuclear weapons, their threat is not only to people ... but also to the earth, the water, the atmosphere and all living things. They can dismantle millions of years of ecological integrity in a matter of minutes.

So, well done to Russia and America for offering to get rid of 30% of their nuclear stockpile. Though, with over a thousand warheads each still remaining, and with the other nuclear powers yet to make a move, there is much dismantling still to be done.

Some people will doubtless see the events of yesterday in Prague as a sign of weakness. They will point to the fact that since Hiroshima there has been no other nuclear bomb exploded for hostile purposes.

That may be so, but one cannot argue that since 1945 the world has been a peaceful place. And maybe, if arms reduction had happened sooner, the threats real or imagined posed by Iraq, Iran and North Korea might never have occurred. We don't know.

But we do know that all the world's great religious and moral teachers concur that might is not always right and that actions which spring from respect and humility make for a longer-lasting good than those which are born of power and arrogance.

9 April 2010

reality TV

Inured to freakery

The Fat Lady was sixpence; so was Tom Thumb and his midget wife. But if my memory serves me right the man with no arms was ninepence because he did something – smoked and shot a rifle with his toes.

Nowadays people open their mouths in disbelief that such mediaeval grotesquery should have been a form of entertainment less than fifty years ago. Righteous indignation would meet any suggestion today that someone who is clinically irregular should be stuck in a tent for the voyeuristic pleasure of the general public.

So why has it taken so long for *Big Brother* to be terminated? A programme which the head of Channel 4 called:

'the most influential show of the modern era'

Certainly, it not only spawned carbon copies elsewhere, but it helped to popularise that genre of programme described by the adjective 'reality', a term which would have George Orwell giving the thumbs up from his grave. It's hard to imagine anything so unreal as a number of hitherto unconnected people being flung together in an alien environment where their interactions are filmed 24 hours a day.

It may seem unfair to compare the freak shows of the past with reality shows of the present. People who appear on *Big Brother* are not solely dependent on it for their livelihood. But I can't help feeling that there is a connection. The base curiosity which led people to pay sixpence to see the Fat Lady is of the same pedigree as that which entices us to watch displays of interpersonal maladjustment.

At least in the past you only looked at the Fat Lady and Tom Thumb on their own. You didn't watch them trying to be compatible.

That human beings have a capacity to be dysfunctional is well attested in sacred scriptures as in secular literature. The mismatch of people living in close proximity is as evident in the story of Samson and Delilah as it is in *EastEnders*.

In a society which is daily confronted with scenes of real or forced degradation, I want to ask what is it that enables us to become noble? What is it that models goodness, not as a soppy sentiment but as a hard choice worth our persevering?

I am constantly amazed that Jesus spends so little time focusing on what is wrong in the world or its people. He doesn't ask for an action replay of aberrant behaviour. So much of his attention is directed to the untapped potential in people and to offering hard options which enable goodness to flourish and society to become just.

Big Brother is said to regularly attract two million viewers. Its proponents will say it caters for an audience. But I doubt if anyone grows one inch in moral stature on what at times can seem like a televisual diet of dysfunction. So, well done Channel 4 for ending *Big Brother*. May whatever replaces it be nourishing as well as entertaining for every little sister.

28th August 2009

remuneration of women

Unfair to a lady

'Why can't a woman be more like a man?' That's a rhetorical question from a revered West End musical. But if answers were an option, someone in the audience might shout, 'Because it would cost too much!'

That certainly would be the case if the fair lady in question were to be one of the gilded few who, having presided before and during the credit crisis, continue to shake hands with themselves and receive massive bonuses in the process. Stephen Hester, the new chief executive of the Royal Bank of Scotland, was reported at the weekend as being the beneficiary of £9.7m from an institution in which the British taxpayer has no small interest and a great deal of capital.

No wonder that last year one in five Oxford graduates ended up in the City.

But how many of them were women?

Ah, there's the rub, as we discovered yesterday when it was revealed that bonuses and sweeteners in the City are prone to gender bias. The findings of a survey by the Equality and Human Rights Commission, which was a substantial project involving almost a quarter of finance sector workers, revealed that female employees earn on average 39% less basic pay than their male counterparts. And when it comes to bonuses, they get around 20% of what might be called masculine supplements.

What is it with women? Are they financially naïve? Are they

busy multitasking when they should be single-mindedly increasing their personal portfolios?

Or is it because the financial industry is still a boy's club?

The industry I represent, if one could call it that, is not innocent of mistreating or even degrading women. The Christian Church has a long history of failing to recognise or encourage female giftedness. Hence most traditional church buildings are rectangular with people sitting in rows facing the man at the front.

As in architecture, so in liturgy. Until very recently, when a woman had a miscarriage or delivered a stillborn child, there were few prayers to represent these particular losses which even yet affect one in four women. Men, who were mostly in charge, didn't make provision for what they couldn't understand.

And this in blatant contradiction to Jesus whose most loyal followers were women, whose prime examples of faith, generosity and love were women, whose first evangelist was a woman, and who even used female illustrations in his talks.

That's partly why they wanted to get rid of him. He was a threat then, as now, to a male hegemony. To heed him is to take all people seriously. It's much easier in the boy's club.

8th September 2008

surveillance

I-spy

It seems that the police use informers.

That, at any rate, is the claim of a member of the ecological protest group Plane Stupid which held a demonstration at Aberdeen airport last month. The person in question alleges that she was approached by an officer from Strathclyde Constabulary and offered money to report on the activities of her group. Shock? Horror?

Well, maybe horror but no shock. The police in every country use informers. One of them used to live with me. He had been involved in paramilitary activities in Northern Ireland, and while he was in prison was offered early release and money if he would inform on the organisation with which he was engaged.

When a danger is posed to the state, the guardians of the law either infiltrate the ranks of the menacing minority or pay insiders to inform on subversive activity.

What do you think of that?

I ask this because I'm not sure myself. On the one hand, it seems a gross infringement of civil liberties for an organisation to be spied on. Does such a practice encourage trust in the police force?

On the other hand, I think of phrases from the lips of Jesus such as, 'You shall know the truth and the truth shall set you free,' or 'What you discuss in secret will be shouted from the rooftops.' If there is a genuine threat to the security of the state and its citizens, is some element of surveillance activity on the part of the security forces not necessary?

Maybe the police should furnish a list of the kind of organisations that are routinely infiltrated, or from whose ranks informers are occasionally seduced by sweeteners.

I mean, given the mess that the country's economy is in because of financial mismanagement, one wonders whether the security forces have allies in Lloyds and RBS. Given the acknowledged high incidence of tax evasion among the super-rich, do the police have informants within those multinational corporations which shunt money from one country to another in order to escape local taxation?

Given the number of people in villages as well as in cities in the UK who are drug addicts, do the police forces have informants in the narcotics and money-laundering spheres who are identifying the Mr Bigs of the illegal drugs trade?

It would be reassuring to know that surveillance is an activity which is as present in the worlds and underworlds of high finance as in the ranks of people who want to save the earth.

Prepared but not broadcast 27 April 09

Indebting the future

At the beginning of January, an article appeared in the reputable *Guardian* newspaper by one of its most prestigious columnists, Max Hastings.

It wasn't a critical tirade against government policy or a scathing indictment of contemporary society. It was almost an *apologia*, a kind of confessional statement about how puzzled this sophisticated journalist was about money. Let me select some of his sentences:

> 'In the past months, the financial meltdown has yielded a flood of global figures that make the nation's domestic budgets seem like small change ...

> 'Beyond grasping we are in a mess, we lack the slightest idea of the significance of the sums of money being pledged, lent, spent or squandered in our name ...

> 'A few months ago it was deemed a scandal that the government was spending £9.3bn ($13bn) of taxpayers' money on the 2012 London Olympics. Now so far have our parameters changed, so drunk on figures have we become, that this sum sounds paltry ...

> 'Perhaps it is a mistake for a newspaper columnist to avow such ignorance about the greatest issue of modern times. But it may make bewildered readers feel better, if a professional pundit occasionally runs up the white flag.'

(*The Guardian*, 5 Jan 09)

I do not want to be presumptuous, but I sense most ordinary citizens of the United Kingdom will probably have been bemused this past twelve months when faced daily with a near-incomprehensible flood of figures and statistics.

What does it mean that Bradford & Bingley should make provision for up to £271m of potential losses through fraud for the first half of this year? Most people, when they look at their bank statement, see clearly if and why they are going into the red. Should a nationalised bank, full of professionals, not be able to spot what is going wrong rather than budget for gross malpractice?

What does it mean that the chancellor should pencil in a £175bn budget deficit this year and the same for next? Given that the nation was asset-stripped in the Thatcher years, what is going to enable the recovery of such an astronomical sum? Or is Mr Darling thinking of pawning the crown jewels?

Such figures are thrown around and we shrug our shoulders or shake our heads in disgust, but rarely do we admit to ourselves or each other that, when it comes to high-octane finance, most of us do not have a clue.

I am reminded of a Glasgow City Councillor called Janey Buchan whom I met about 30 years ago when I was in student politics. Janey had just been at a meeting of the Council's Education Committee and the smoke was coming out of her ears.

She said, in terms which I am editing to avoid offending sensitivities:

'I cannot believe what we have just done.

'We spent 50 minutes discussing whether we should upgrade two typewriters for hardworking secretaries, and give them electric rather than manual machines. It was going to cost us about £120 all in. After 50 minutes we decided against it.

'Next business was whether we should refurbish a school
swimming pool for £250,000.
We passed that on the nod.'

So I asked her why she thought that so much time was taken
to discuss and then reject the proposal for the office and yet in
no time at all the work on the swimming pool was approved.

She said,

'I suppose it's because we all have an idea of how much a
typewriter costs.
So we argue about it.
But when it comes to a quarter of a million pounds of
work on a pool, we haven't a clue.'

This sense of inadequacy admitted by Max Hastings was
more recently endorsed by another journalist, Hadley
Freeman, who said regarding the trial and imprisonment of
Bernie Madoff, the billionaire embezzler:

'Now that he's languishing in jail, it's clear why Madoff
got away with it for so long: no one understands finance.'
(*The Guardian* 15/07/09)

If, for the majority of citizens, the financial malaise around us
seems to have no proven beginning, guaranteed end, or iden-
tifiable direction of travel, there is little that the Christian
churches seem to be able to offer apart from prayers for the
well-being of the victims of redundancy and recession.

I don't imagine many pastors will have prayed:

'that the culprits in striped suits might be identified,
that those who have lost out might be remunerated

and that those who have made fast bucks will be turned empty away'

... in the style of Mary's Magnificat.

I don't imagine many bishops will have peppered their talks to the Rotary Club with quotations from the book of Amos such as:

'Some of you have turned justice itself into poison.'
(Amos 6:12)

Nor do I imagine that the well coiffured and impeccably dressed preachers who appear in the mega-churches will encourage congregations hooked on success-theology to ponder proverbs at bedtime such as:

'What use is money in the hands of a fool?
Can he buy wisdom if he has no sense?'
(Proverbs 17:16)

Christians, by and large, have been reticent to speak of money, apart from encouraging people to tithe. This silence, as we will discover, is out of kilter with biblical witness. But before looking at Scripture, a little regression therapy.

Voices from the past

As Samuel in the Old Testament is remembered for responding to a voice speaking to him while yet young, we all will have words from our adolescent or teenage years which still reverberate in us.

Some of these will have been spoken by teachers; but there are other – perhaps less professional but equally important

– voices which address us over the years, like that of my grandmother:

> 'Pay your rent, insurance and food
> and see everything else as a bonus.'

And also

> 'Never buy what you can't afford
> and don't get into debt.'

She had lived through the depression of the '30s with two children, an unemployed husband and, for a while, two nieces, all of whom lived in a room of no more than about 30 square yards with one cold tap and an outside toilet. She had one chest of drawers, three deep, and a wardrobe in which everyone's clothes were kept.

There was nothing in her experience which threatened her life in any direct way except for poverty or a possible invasion by Germany.

Personal experience

When I left school in 1968 to go to university, I held dear to my grandmother's maxims.

I came from a low-income family, so I was awarded a full student grant from the government, the princely sum of £90 per term of 10 weeks. And with this I paid my rent, bought my books, purchased food and had enough money to assure at least one night of socialising at the weekend.

I had no bank card, just a bank book which I would take weekly to the Trustee Savings Bank to withdraw my rent money and living expenses. Later I acquired a cheque book and on one occasion was summoned to the bank to account for myself because I was overdrawn by £2.40.

I left university after six years' study with no debt and, along with a friend, bought a three-roomed flat for around £6,500 on a maximum mortgage that was less than my annual salary.

The only contemporary threat to my life, of which I was aware, was the possibility of nuclear war initiated by Russia or the USA. At that time, not 20 miles from Glasgow, there was the largest nuclear silo in the free world with both British and American naval bases hidden in adjacent Scottish lochs.

Students today

I now live in a country where present and former government ministers who, as students, benefited from a generous grant and bursary system, have overseen the expansion of higher education and the change from grants to loans, such that any young person going to university might expect after three years to be indebted to the sum of £20,000 or more.

They live in a world where neither the poverty my grandmother feared nor the nuclear war I feared are liable to affect them.

But in years to come they will live in a world where the presumed privilege of the English-speaking North will be decimated by the justifiable reconfiguration of global power to favour the industrial East of India and China, and the emerging economies of Central and Southern America.

More to the point, they may face the potential end of the world as we know it through one of these phenomena:

> pollution,
> global warming
> mismanagement of natural resources leading to food
> shortages
> OR – who knows? –
> war which might result from the West wilfully refusing
> to change its highly consumerist lifestyle.

In the past year, I have been invited twice to address the sixth forms of prestigious high schools, one in Glasgow and one in Oxford, about the use and abuse of money. These engagements have been among the most difficult I have ever undertaken, because in speaking about these issues, you cannot responsibly disguise the bottom line – namely, to paraphrase John the Baptist,

> We must decrease
> that others might increase.

The world cannot sustain our lifestyle. We are on the brink of indebting the future not only with a financial burden but with an existential burden which nothing and no one will be able to eradicate, apart from God. And all the indications in scripture are that God does not prevent people from falling into a trap they have knowingly laid for themselves.

Let's take three very different examples of this indebtedness:

If you have never seen the film *China Blue*, try to do so. It is a documentary about life in a Chinese factory which produces denim jeans. It is horrifying to see the conditions in which workers live (in a hostel adjacent to the factory). It is horrifying to see the risk to their health from both machinery and the toxic chemicals with which they work. There are also other phenomena which make the viewer recoil in disgust.

But the vilest thing comes at the end, when a British importer is filmed talking to the factory owner who, to be fair, does not seem like a money-grabbing exploiter. When asked the cost of the jeans, the owner says he could sell them at around $2.40 (£2.00 a pair). The British importer says he could never sell them at that price, so negotiates with – or rather bullies – the owner until he gets the jeans at under £2.00. He will then retail them for between 6 and 10 times that amount, in order that he can make a tidy profit and the British public can have cheap clothing.

That is what we expect isn't it? Cheap clothing: T-shirts for £1.50 out of Asda, shirts for under £10 in H&M. And if the price isn't low enough, we can wait until the sales.

Sometimes people complain that the proliferation of charity shops in certain neighbourhoods is a sign of poverty. It is nothing of the kind. It is a sign of affluence, of how we have so many shirts and jeans which are so cheap to come by that, rather than wear them out, we give them to Oxfam.

You don't get charity shops stocked from the cast-offs of people living in areas of multiple deprivation; you get them in the proximity of affluent neighbourhoods.

The world cannot afford us to exercise our assumed right to cheap clothing at the expense of underpaid labourers.

We are indebting the future.

My second illustration comes from *The Herald* (a Scottish newspaper) on Sunday 23rd August 2009. It concerns how cod caught off the shores of Scotland is being shipped 10,000 miles to and from China in order that food processors who earn less than £1.00 per day can prepare it for the return journey to British tables. Prawns and langoustines are also the subjects of this global transportation.

Apart from the wrong-headedness of deliberately engaging people who are paid a fraction of our national minimum wage to do work which could be done equally well in Britain, think of the cost to the environment. But this is not an isolated example. It is now commonplace for air transport to bring organic onions from Chile to Britain, or flowers from North Africa to Covent Garden, or bottled water from Fiji to Harvey Nichols.

This is an aspect of a new kind of exploitation (land and commodity imperialism) which, according to the United Nations, has seen wealthy countries like Japan, the Gulf States, Russia and even Sweden appropriate around 30m hectares of foreign land (half the size of Europe) in order to grow cheap food which is flown in to preserve its freshness. (*The Guardian*, 4 July 09)

The world cannot afford us to exercise our assumed right to cheap food at the expense of the environment.

We are indebting the future.

My third illustration simply requires us to think of the sky-line of the City of London. Where once the Old Lady of Threadneedle Street ruled supreme, now there are buildings which tower high above the Bank of England, buildings which house firms of accountants, international financiers and lawyers who are accountable to no one and, as was evident with the debacle in the Royal Bank of Scotland, whose shareholders are fed only the information which management thinks is palatable.

These are the financially 'sussed' people who have caused the developing world to lose $1trn this year through the global recession, of which some were prime movers. These are people like the flash salesmen of Barclays Bank, which in 2004 was exposed for making billions out of encouraging people to buy unnecessary add-on insurances to mortgages and loans. But when the credit crunch came, were these surplus billions put at the disposal of their debtors or those whose pension schemes had crashed and whose savings had disappeared?

Yet this same bank, as reported in June of this year, is happy to pay bonuses of up to £55m to its already super-wealthy executives. (*The Guardian* 19 & 22 June 09 & *Rich Britain* p90)

These are the people whom the government is afraid to rein in, for fear that they leave Britain and take their contacts with them. But, I fondly ask, which country in the civilised world would want to employ financial managers who have brought about ruin while lining their own pockets? In his book *Rich Britain*, Stewart Lansley comments:

'There is no evidence of a brain drain to the USA.
There remains little demand for UK executives overseas;
In fact the traffic has mostly been in the other direction.'
(*Rich Britain* p96)

The economist JK Galbraith made an interesting comment on the rash of self-aggrandisement from which the world has so recently suffered:

'The salary of the chief executive of the larger corporation is *not* a market award for achievement. It is frequently in the nature of a warm personal gesture by the individual to himself.'
(*Rich Britain* p97)

But back to the buildings ...

What do they produce? Emails and effluent. There are no marketable goods which emerge from these huge edifices. They do not manufacture commodities that can be sold. They do not physically increase the nation's export capacity. These giant hothouses do not even grow tomatoes for the domestic market.

The year before the credit crunch, the entire financial sector delivered £12.4bn in corporation tax. But this has to be set beside the figure of £141bn which the Office for National Statistics has identified as the amount of money expended by the government in the attempt to steady the financial markets. Yet such information, which questions the integrity of the City, does not diminish its allure.

The pay and conditions are immensely attractive to the upwardly mobile, so much so that last year one in five Oxford graduates went to the City, including engineering graduates whose skills were allegedly honed in academia for physical construction rather than fiscal avoidance.

At the time when productive factories are being threatened with closure and subsequent demolition (such as Johnny Walker's in my home town of Kilmarnock, and Bausch & Lomb in Livingston) the City of London continues to erect monuments to financial avarice which will house employees whose primary concern is to play or control the money markets.

The world cannot afford a privileged and unaccountable cabal of international financiers to withdraw and deposit money as suits their self-interest, irrespective of the cost to the global economy and particularly the poor.

We are indebting the future.

But there is one other thing which the world cannot afford, and that is for Christians to exempt themselves from the discussion just because they can't tell the difference between the Dow Jones Index and a knitting pattern. Nor can Christians get away with the notion that money is not God's business and therefore our minds should be on things of a higher plane.

In the interests of time, I am going to forgo a survey of where and how often the five books of Moses, the Proverbs, the Psalms and the Prophets deal repeatedly and perceptively with money. Suffice it to say that if one were to draw a conclusion from the extensive references to money in the Hebrew scriptures it would be that money cannot be separated from morality.

Jesus, money and morality

Christians belong to perhaps the most materialistic of all religions, because Christianity claims that the invisible God became matter, and in handling money (as undoubtedly Jesus did), and in drawing attention to its potentials (as he also did), Christ makes clear that personal and global finances are issues of faith. It is regrettable that, unlike Jesus, Christians have been so reticent to engage with this issue.

Unlike some of his followers then and now, Jesus had no difficulty in speaking about money.

He was perfectly at home in the houses of the wealthy. There were several sympathetic or curious Pharisees who invited him to dinner. And there were Joanna and Susanna, two women who were married to affluent civil servants, who provided him and his disciples with food and lodging. It was no embarrassment for him to be in such company.

But note that he did not enjoy the company of the wealthy just so that he could berate them. He never turned up like a tramp at posh dinner parties to make his hosts feel guilty, although when it came to naming the dangers of excessive affluence, he had no hesitation.

We tend to think of him as coming from the poorest of backgrounds because he was born in a manger. That was not a sign of poverty. It was an indication of how busy Bethlehem was. If we have to put Jesus in a class, he would probably be lower middle, given his presumed career as a self-employed carpenter or, more likely, builder.

The proof that he had no difficulty in being with the wealthy or talking about money can be gleaned by his fondness for the subject in many of his parables such as:

> The Prodigal Son
> The Good Samaritan
> The Guests Invited to the Banquet
> The Talents
> The Men Hired in the Market Place
> The Ungrateful Servant
> The Lost Coin
> Dives and Lazarus.

Nearly all of Jesus' parables deal with either money or food, yet amazingly we tend to think of him as one whose waistline was nearer 26 inches than 34, and as someone who was financially naïve.

Is it because he asked for a coin to be shown when confronted with the demand to talk about taxes that we imagine he never handled hard cash? Or are we projecting onto him our own hesitancy and ambivalence towards money?

I cannot give a blueprint for financial rectitude on either a personal or a national level. I am not an economist, but I think there are certain issues that Christians can address that would enable us to be more confident in dealing with that financial malaise which might equally be called a global pandemic.

1) Demonisation of money

We have to stop demonising money, because as long as we refuse to address financial issues openly, we take money out of the realm of morality, and we accord it a privileged status granted to nothing else.

Think of how people speak of the commodity:

> Filthy lucre
> Dirty money
> Risky/dodgy business
> Backhanders
> Black market
> Underground economy
> Creative accounting
> Slush funds
> Shady deals

It all sounds as if money is something that is intrinsically tainted. When we speak of it as such, it becomes easier to engage in shoddy deals, to speculate with an eye to causing havoc on the money markets, or to indulge in less high-octane but equally dubious activities. It is comparable to how men, who presume women to be the 'seducers', rationalise away extra-marital affairs on the grounds that 'this is the kind of thing that happens when you're confronted with that sort of woman'.

A while ago I went into my local travel agent to get a plane ticket. I was offered one on a budget airline for about £45. The travel agent offered to give me a receipt for £200. I asked why and he said, 'A lot of businessmen do this. The company doesn't need to know you got a bargain.' He thought he was doing me a favour by encouraging me to swindle £150 from my employers.

I want to assert that money is a good thing. It should not be regarded as something intrinsically evil. In itself it is morally neutral. The way in which it is used or misused is what accords it, or rather its handlers, ethical standing or opprobrium.

Let me assure you that there is nowhere in the Bible, and certainly not in the teaching of Jesus, that money is considered to be suspect. Jesus has no fear of handling or discussing it.

But, equally, he has no fear of confronting the misuse of currency, as when in the parables of Dives and Lazarus and the Rich Fool he pronounces a negative judgement on those whose wealth is used solely for personal aggrandisement. A better-known example would be his scandalous upturning of the moneychangers' seats in the Temple, an action born of anger, the root of which is not personal animosity or jealousy, but a passionate antipathy to financial chicanery which adversely affects the poor and the outsider.

The fact that money in Christian circles is usually associated with the need to repair leaking roofs or increase charitable giving is totally misrepresentative of its importance to Christ. Indeed I would claim that if we ceased to demonise money and were as easy in speaking of it as Jesus was, there would be fewer leaking roofs and no hesitation about charitable giving, for we would see the potential of money to be part of God's redeeming purpose.

In the past, when society was differently ordered, we relied overmuch on the philanthropy of the wealthy. Those days are gone. The fact that the generosity of Bill Gates is frequently mentioned has as much to do with his being a rare species as it has to do with his beneficence. Surveys of today's super-wealthy indicate that the more money people have, the less generous proportionally they become.

2) Bad-mouthing of taxation

We have developed in Britain an irrational aversion to taxation, and commonly speak of it as an unnecessary intrusion which has to be avoided at all costs.

Yet we cannot have a good health system with equal access for all irrespective of income if there is insufficient tax revenue. We cannot have a good transport system which enables people to travel quickly nationwide on trains, thus preventing atmospheric pollution by planes, without investment capital raised through taxation. We cannot equip our defence forces so that they are adequate for the tasks expected of them without finance proportionally collected from the citizens of the nation whose defence they maintain.

I earn around £24,000 per annum. I am a single man, so I have no tax allowances. I am taxed at the maximum. But I would gladly pay more tax if I believed that it would go to fund the activities just mentioned, and to feed the hungry, clothe the naked and take care of the poor. I see it as a privilege to pay tax, not a curse.

And I do this because I cannot see anywhere in scripture where *justifiable* taxation is condemned. *Unjustifiable* yes, and there is plenty of evidence in the prophets and the book of

Proverbs of how God inveighs against burdensome taxes. Indeed, in the book of Judges there is a story I enjoy sharing with children about a big fat king called Egol who is exacting unfair taxes from the Jews. So God identifies a left-handed man to change the situation (3:15-25).

His name is Ehud, and after presenting the taxes to the king, he asks if he can speak to him in private. The king sends away his attendants and rises to his feet when Ehud says,

'I have a message from God for you.'

As the king rises to receive the message, Ehud puts his left hand over to his right, pulls out a sword and sticks it through the fat king's belly. The fat closes over the hilt of the blade and because it goes right through him, stuff comes out the back which it is not polite to talk about. Ehud locks the door of the king's chamber and runs off. The attendants presume that the king must be taking his time in the toilet. After a while, fearing he is suffering from terminal constipation, they break down the door and find their master lying dead on the floor.

Now, among many possible reasons for that story being in scripture, one is that God does not favour unjust taxation.

In the Gospels, Jesus' attitude to tax is explicit. He is asked by Peter whether they should pay local taxes and he says, 'Yes' (Matthew 17:27). He enjoys spending time in the company of tax collectors far more than in that of priests. He consents to people paying their dues to the Roman authorities ('give to Caesar what is Caesar's').

This biblical witness is *not* attested when people of faith nod their heads or stamp their feet any time politicians promise that, if they are elected, they will lower taxes. Go to the USA and see the consequences of low-tax regimes: forty-seven million people who cannot afford health insurance and live in fear of being ill, and the hurricane devastation in Louisiana even yet being repaired not by Federal funding but by the generosity of churches and other charitable organisations.

3) Experiencing the benefits of accountability

The Iona Community to which I belong requires, as part of its discipline, that all members account for our use of money. We have a commitment to give away 10% of our disposable income and to talk with each other both about how we disburse our tithe and about what we do with the 90% we retain. We do this in small groups once a year, and for most of us this is the most liberating of conversations, probably because we operate from the premise that money is neutral in itself but has a value imposed on it by the way we use it.

If our use of this public commodity is going to be a secret thing, then irresponsibility and recklessness can have a field day. But if our use of this public commodity is something which can be spoken of positively and confidently, then creative things can happen. I say a *public commodity* because this is what distinguishes money from two other issues which have a high risk rating on the religious conversation list, sex and death. These latter are primarily matters of private morality; money is primarily a matter of public ethics.

Those who are on the breadline or on social security cannot be secretive about their wealth. The minimum wage and the rate of welfare payments are known and the state agencies are obliged to investigate personal sources of income before deciding the benefits to which a claimant may be entitled. Additionally, if you are unemployed you are likely to talk with other disadvantaged people about how you survive on dole money.

Should those who are wealthy not also be able to have such conversations? The experience of my community is that when such a conversation happens, both poor and wealthy benefit. There are pressures on the financially disadvantaged which the more privileged cannot understand. But equally there are pressures on high earners to embark on an upward spiral of unnecessarily lavish living which it is hard to resist unless there is a forum in which the use of personal finances can be discussed.

There is a 'condition' to which social scientists have given the name Affluenza. If I were less of a Luddite, I would have a screen on which to show a graph which has Fulfilment on the vertical and Consumption on the horizontal. It indicates that 'enough is enough' happens at a point between living in comfort and living in luxury. When that point is passed, consumption increases exponentially, as does unhappiness.

We have no difficulty in feeling it our Christian duty to prevent people from living in penury. If we realise that both penury and luxury are bad for the human soul, should we not have a similar duty to prevent people from entering the zone of abject luxury?

In all this, the key issue is to redeem the currency, to recognise that money is not dirty or filthy or seductive per se. If we believe that the earth is the Lord's, then money is also the Lord's and we should be able as Christians to speak honestly and to be accountable for how we deal with this resource.

This I believe to be wholly consonant with the Gospel.

Global responsibility and corporate financial accountability

But Christians who feel a concern about wealth and poverty in God's world cannot simply see financial accountability as a personal matter. We must also be engaged in ensuring that financial accountability happens across the board, and particularly in the world of high finance.

That there are companies which have bigger turnovers than the GDP of some nation states has long been accepted. But who keeps such corporations in check in the same way that the World Bank and IMF scrutinise the finances of developing nations?

A reader of *The Sun* newspaper in Britain has no option but to pay tax because it is deducted from his or her wage packet at source. But, if he or she were found to be earning excessive amounts of undeclared income, or worse, to be earning money while signing on the dole, *The Sun* would have a field-day. Is the owner of *The Sun* so assiduous in his own compliance with fiscal measures?

The Murdoch empire is a magnificent example of, among other things, tax avoidance. The journalist Stewart Lansley in his book *Rich Britain* makes the damning comment that:

> 'Rupert Murdoch's media empire has paid hardly anything in tax since the late '70s. His News Corporation consists of a web of 800 subsidiaries, many of them registered in offshore tax havens.

> 'A study of the 101 subsidiaries operational in Britain revealed that in an 11 year period they had profits of £1.4 billion, but curiously had paid minimal corporation tax.' (*Rich Britain* p187)

107

The appalling thing about this is that, if the allegedly born-again Murdoch is able to practise such avoidance and get away with it, it is an encouragement to lesser mortals to seek the same kind of scheming exemption. Lansley again:

> 'By hiring the best legal and accountancy brains, it is possible to exploit tax loopholes in a way that makes paying tax a largely voluntary act.' (*Rich Britain* p197)

Equally the salaries and sweeteners of those who control the money of millions have to be open to public scrutiny. If people insist on scaling the heights of high finance for their personal gain, then they should forfeit that same gain if they are found culpable of neglect.

Recently the chairman of the World Bank was reported as saying that as a consequence of the credit crunch which devastated Wall St in New York, he expected that an extra 44 million people in the developing world would become malnourished. This is in addition to over 900 miliion who are already starving. It is not just the shareholders who are hurting. Their pain is financial, not mortal.

And so I would claim that if for a moment we imagine that the global issues to which I refer are not the substance of faith, not matters of concern within the church, then we are being dishonest with God and disrespectful to the Gospel in which our Saviour is repeatedly depicted as one who ensured that all were fed and whose self-stated purpose was to bring good news to the poor.

Whenever in this joined-up and information-soaked world we deal with money, we are making moral choices. And that is not just a matter of deciding to give donations to the Leprosy Mission or Save the Children rather than buy another unneeded electrical gadget. Such a decision is an ethical choice which can help to enhance the life of vulnerable people. But it is not the only kind of ethical choice.

For when I buy a product sourced from abroad at a price which guarantees that the producer and his or her family will not benefit from a fair wage, I am making a moral decision to keep people in poverty.

When my appetite for ready-meals involving beef sees me regularly purchasing such produce from Asda, Tesco and Marks & Spencer's, not only am I making a moral decision to encourage the development of the cattle industry, which is a major methane producer, but I am also assenting to the deforestation of the Amazon and the subsequent effect on the ecosphere and the livelihoods of indigenous peoples.

When I decide to stock my cupboards with more food than I know I will use, I am making a moral decision to add in my own small way to Britain's mountain of waste. According to Tristam Stuart in his book *Waste: Uncovering the Global Food Scandal*,

> 'The 61,300 tonnes of tomatoes people in the UK throw into their waste bins are produced by the same amount of energy as it takes to grow enough wheat to relieve the hunger of 105m people.' (Quoted in *The Guardian Review* 01/08/09)

If I work for a company where my expense account is a bottomless purse and my expenses are never queried, and the expectation is that will I fly everywhere and hire a car at my destination rather than use public transport or a taxi, I am making a moral decision to add to the pollution of the globe. I may be in favour of a greener environment, but my actions suggest that other people should pay for it.

Yet this is not intended to be a litany of gloom. For the reality is that when people turn the corner to become more financially accountable, then guilt and the denial of responsibility for global injustice are dissipated.

When people know that redistribution of wealth, a beneficent lifestyle and the confrontation of financial injustice and mismanagement yield positive results, there is the growth of a very real conviction that this is the work of God's kingdom. I believe that the enthusiasm for the Jubilee 2000 campaign affecting debt relief, and the more recent interest in the 10:10 campaign in favour of reduction of carbon emissions, are indices of how underneath our avarice there is a desire for altruism to blossom.

Standard of living

But I come back to the bottom line which confronts me whenever I speak to teenagers, namely that the world cannot afford us. We cannot presume that our standard of living can continue while people elsewhere somehow compensate for our avarice. And we certainly cannot bring up our children to believe that the comparative wealth they enjoy is their perennial birthright.

Through buying into a consumerist culture we have effectively substituted having for being, possession for achievement, purchasing for entertainment.

Teenagers from the 1990s onwards have increasingly become the objects of the predatory interests of the moguls of the fashion, music and culture industries. Aware of the changeable nature of the adolescent mind, the sales-pitch for 'desirable' commodities perpetually offers this or that gadget or accessory as a 'must-have'. Where in the '70s punks and hippies made a virtue out of recycling or minimising clothing and espousing a non-commercial cultural milieu, their contemporary counterparts do not feel neat on the street unless designer clothes and the latest technological communication gadgetry are hanging about their persons.

But here they may merely be emulating their parents who, buoyed up on an illusory credit wave, acquiesced to all manner of extravagance to compensate for dull lives.

Purchasing as surrogate entertainment may seem an unusual conjecture. But all studies of people who are binge shoppers indicate that those who indulge themselves in department stores on a regular basis have little appreciation for what they purchase. What they enjoy is the thrill of spending money, just as a gambler gets a rush when he or she puts money on the gaming table.

There is an illogical side to this, which perhaps authenticates binge shopping as more of a disorder than a habit. You may fill your wardrobe with clothes, but you can still only wear one shirt or dress at a time. You may cram your sitting room with expensive ornaments, but your eyes gradually become inured to the presumed uniqueness of the latest purchase from a fashionable accessories store.

We, who follow Jesus, follow someone who repeatedly and explicitly pointed to relationships with God, with each other, and with the earth as the primary sources of depth and fulfilment. When our primary passions are those of possession and consumption, not only do we require the despoiling of the earth and a plundering of its resources to buttress Western lifestyles, but we also diminish the possibility of our growing as human beings by being enchanted by the earth, delighted by its inhabitants, and edified by God whose channels of mercy are always real people and the physical world, never plastic or commercial substitutes.

There will be people who read these words who are much more sophisticated in their understanding of money than I am. I would urge them to be bold and articulate in allowing their faith to inform their financial practices and judgements. And I would encourage them to share their wisdom in their communities of faith.

For the rest of us, whom telephone-figure salaries and the FTSE leave bemused, I suggest that neither God nor the world can wait much longer for us to lose our reticence and loosen our tongues.

Since God took flesh in Jesus Christ, the material world and what benefits or threatens it cannot be left to a select few. For all Christians, matter matters. The phrase, *'money makes the world go round'* would become less of a lyric and more of truism if we would only speak of it more freely.

Footnote: This paper was delivered first at Greenbelt Festival and later, in a revised form, as the Joseph Winter Lecture in Leeds. On both occasions, and much to my surprise, innumerable people made the comment that this was the first time in a Christian context that they had heard the subject of money offered for public discussion.

The love of God and global warming

We will all have a different story about what either alerted us to the reality of global warming or convinced us of its severity. For some people it might have been a statistic that stuck in the mind, for others an image in a newspaper. For others yet it might have been seeing Al Gore's uncompromising yet hopeful film, *An Inconvenient Truth*.

A journey in unseasonable weather

For me it was a journey, one which took in four continents and a variety of cities, and in each place unseasonable weather.

The first stop for Christmas was Kathmandu in Nepal, a Hindu kingdom where I have a friend who is an evangelist in an indigenous church. The weather was unseasonable, too warm for that time of year. It had the effect of making visitors like myself want to shower regularly, something also encouraged by the smog from old motorcars, motorbikes and mopeds.

But Nepal cannot afford more people wanting water in the winter. It already has enough difficulty coping with the needs of tourists in the summer. Fresh water is in short supply. As the Himalayan glaciers melt at an ever-increasing rate, the amount of water available to Nepal gradually diminishes.

For New Year, I was in Auckland and watched a clearly disappointing midnight fireworks display in the central square. The weather was muggy, the sky misted over. The next day, in a local shoe shop, the owner spoke of how New Year as he remembered it was always a time of bright skies, clear light and fun at the beach. The last ten years had brought heat, but not too much by way of sunlight.

Then it was the Upper Clarence region of New South Wales in Australia. The town was Casino, once the beef capital of the continent. But not any longer. I met farmers whose herds had suffered so much from drought that they were shooting the cattle, burying them and then trying to sell land on which nothing could now be reared.

Over to Toronto in early February. The city was just recovering from its heaviest snow fall in decades. So much snow fell that the troops had to be brought in to clear it from the streets into the lake.

Fearing that Wheaton College in Illinois might also be snowed in, I phoned the professor I was to work with and asked him for a weather check. He looked out of his window and said that, unseasonably for that time of year, most of the male students were walking about in shorts and T-shirts.

When I arrived back in Europe, I went to the Netherlands where the weather was seasonal, but where people were concerned about recent conjectures that global warming might cause sufficient of the polar ice-cap to melt for the sea-level to rise and threaten nations like the Netherlands, parts of which are already below sea-level.

But is it a faith issue?

While global warming might be an existential threat, is it a legitimate subject for religious faith? I mean, when did anyone last hear a biblically-based sermon on meteorology, and who ever wrote or sang hymns about the depletion of the ozone layer?

I want to claim that this is a profoundly biblical issue and its lamentable absence from the preaching or teaching of the church may in part be due to the historic legacy of the theologies of sages such as Augustine and Calvin who were more concerned with the errant nature of humanity than with the environment entrusted to humanity's care by God. But, to be fair, one also has to admit that neither Augustine nor Calvin were creatures of the industrial revolution which was the starting point for the systematic despoliation of the earth and its ecosystem.

Historical theology apart, issues of ecology have not enjoyed the attention they deserve, because they are innately controversial. As we shall discover later, to move from admiring sunsets to owning responsibility for drought in the Sahel is, in liturgical terms, to move from adoration to confession and that is not as popular as it once was. More particularly, any realistic response to issues of climate change and ecological mismanagement impinge directly on the style of life which we in the West presume to be our birthright. And no one likes being asked to surrender privilege, especially when there is nothing by way of immediate compensation.

Here I want to offer four biblical perspectives on God, nature and humanity.

Four biblical perspectives

1) Nature has an *anima* as well as an *animus*

... but we are more inclined to think of the latter rather than the former. *Animus* is the display of terror which we see unleashed in irregular weather patterns such as the 2004 Indian Ocean tsunami or the freak storms and high seas which destroyed New Orleans.

We perceive this animus, this malign activity of nature, in the failure of the weather to deliver the goods we believe we deserve. Thus several years ago much of the population of lowland Scotland suffered from congestive disorders because we 'had not had a good frost to kill the germs'. Meanwhile the ski slopes of the Grampian Highlands languished through a lack of the snow which resort owners and skiers believed was their winter due.

This punitive depiction (some might call it demonisation) of nature has to do with a wider and deeper perception of the earth and the whole ecosystem, which has been inherited through the ages with the help of the aforementioned theologians who tended to reify nature, treating it as a thing to be mastered and an enemy when it failed to comply.

What has been lost is the much more profound and certainly more biblical perception of nature not as animus but as *anima*, an entity with an inner personality.

And when something has an inner personality, you don't bend it to your will, you enter into a relationship with it. You do not treat it to what social psychologists call 'moral exclusion'. The relationship between nature and humanity has to be interdependent. God recognises this, as do the most discerning of poets and prophets. And the Bible bears ample witness.

a) Unusual terminology?

There are some verses in the Bible which, taken in isolation, could come from a new-age compendium:

> 'The valleys stand so full of corn, they laugh and sing.'
> (Ps 65:13)

'Let the rivers clap their hands, let the mountains sing together.' (Ps 98:8)

'The hills skip like rams and the little hills like lambs.' (Ps 114:4)

Were anyone to go for a stroll and announce on returning that he or she had just heard the river nearby clapping its hands and seen the hills skipping, the rambler might be suspected of having ingested something considerably stronger than coffee. But essentially this biblical language is expressing a view of creation as something which is shot through with animation and emotion, rather than attractive but placid like an illustration on a chocolate box.

b) Direct divine address

But more than this, the created order is that to which God relates as personally as God relates to the Chosen People of the Hebrew scriptures, or the New Testament Church. Creation is addressed by God and is the plaything and delight of God.

'God not only lays the earth's foundations, but fathers the rain, gives the horse its energy and teaches the hawk how to use its pinions.' (Job 38 & 39)

'God knows every bird and hence is aware when even a common sparrow falls to the ground.' (Psalm 50:11/Matthew 10:29)

Because the earth stands in a personal relationship to God, the earth is the object of direct address, to which it is expected to respond, not out of fear, but out of fondness:

'Let the sea resound, the world and its inhabitants.' (Psalm 98:7)

'Let the desert rejoice and flower, let it rejoice and shout for joy.' (Isaiah 35:1)

Humanity may not be able to understand this conversation, it may even mock the mere notion of it, but the prophets call humanity back to a listening rather than a presumptive role, for they know that God speaks to nature. Hence Ezekiel:

'O man, prophesy to the mountains and say: Mountains of Israel, hear the word of the Lord.' (Ezekiel 36:1)

or Micah:

'Hear the Lord's case, you mountains; he has a case against his people.' (Micah 6:2)

In this last quotation, God is using nature as an ally and a witness against humanity, because the earth is a much older friend of God than Adam and his descendants. The earth was singing a love song to its Maker long before humanity was conceived.

c) The whole earth paean

This alludes to a third aspect of the relational bond between God and the earth, namely that the earth is a forum of worship as magnificent and intricate as the wildest dreams of the most sophisticated liturgist.

If one asks the Bible why did God create the earth, the answer is not: in order that humanity might have a habitation. The answer is: in order that God might enjoy it.

There is a mystical symphony constantly being improvised by creation to which our ears are not attuned, because we are so used to music being a human artefact.

119

The rhythm section has to do with the regularity and irregularity of tides and times and season. I say the irregularity, because that is part of the skill we admire in Ghanaian drummers. Rhythm is not always strictly ballroom.

The orchestral voices muster the delicacy of birdsong and the rumbustiousness of the tempest. And not everything harmonises all the time, because the best composers from Bach to Billy Joel know how dull music can be if, like some classical music radio stations, it aims always to be 'soothing'. Tension, clash, unpredictable changes in pitch and volume provide excitement.

And God is the audience who watches and listens to and admires and applauds this song of creation in which 'night to night imparts knowledge, and this without any speech or language'. (Psalm 19)

Humanity's responsibility is not to interfere with the music. From a biblical perspective it is as reprehensible and profane an activity to interfere with the playing of this improvised paean of creation as it would be to lace the throats of a cathedral choir with superglue. All ancient civilisations recognise this. It is what makes for an amazing consonance in the spiritual traditions of, to name only a few, Aboriginal Australians, the indigenous First Nations of Canada and the ancient British Celts. That is why, for example, at the public hearing against the proposal to dig a superquarry on the island of Harris, one of the plaintiffs against the proposal was a Canadian First Nations' leader. Those closest to the earth know there are songlines which should not be broken.

The civilised and the urbanised and the Bible-readers who believe that God's primary focus is the welfare of their private souls don't get it. But one unlikely man did.

He was a tradesman I met in Bradwell-on-Sea, in Essex.

I had spoken earlier that day at a pilgrimage to an ancient Celtic site on a promontory not far from the village. I met him in the pub in the evening. He told me of his antipathy to religion, but also of how sometimes he would walk alone to the ancient chapel and sit outside it and watch the sea and the birds and listen to the ambience of it all. And he said, 'Despite myself, I believe there is something there.'

Years previously, I might have suggested that he was 'communing with God, but did not realise it'. I am glad I offered no such bland interpretation. Now I am convinced that, albeit unarticulated by him, he was present when nature was offering to God its worship, and he was fulfilling the divine mandate requiring humanity not to interfere.

2) Dominion is not domination

The second perspective I want to suggest is that the relationship between earth and humanity should be that of dominion and not domination. It is, after all, dominion which God, in Genesis Chapter 1, bestows as a privilege and responsibility on the first humans.

If you want to know the difference between the two, then think of Canada. It started being a dominion when Britain stopped dominating it.

The Bible, in its prophetic and poetic literature, makes quite clear that there is an intrinsic connection between the earth's failing to deliver the goods and humanity's failing to behave responsibly.

We sometimes talk about people who are indiscreet or presumptuous in interpersonal relationships as 'not respecting the boundaries'. The same applies to our collective relationship with and to creation.

Where there is a breach, it is always on the part of humanity. Thus Jeremiah:

> 'Your wrongdoing has upset nature's order and your sins have kept away her bounty.' (Jer. 5:25)

And again:

> 'You defiled the land ... therefore showers were withheld and rain failed.' (Jer. 43:2-3)

Then from Haggai:

> 'It is your fault that the heavens withhold their moisture and the earth its produce.' (Hagg 1:10)

And, most graphically, Isaiah:

> 'The earth lurches like a drunkard, the sins of its inhabitants weigh heavy on it; it falls to rise no more.'
> (Isaiah 24.20)

Though we were not present, there was a contractual agreement, known as a covenant, drawn up in the founding days of humanity on earth. It is published at the end of that amusing story of Noah and the Ark. A flood had covered the earth because God wanted to bring humanity down to size. But there is a regret in the heart of God, because it was not simply humanity which was affected by the deluge. The flood, like a nuclear bomb, affected land, animals, water and air as well as humans.

So in the covenant that God makes with Noah after the flood, God promises never to engineer such a thing again. As a sign God puts the rainbow in the sky. We see it as a colourful meteorological phenomenon but its symbolic value is quite different. The bow is the symbol of God's power to dominate. Therefore God leaves the bow in the sky as an adornment to creation, which like an ancient cannon in a museum will, by dint of its locus, never be used for malevolent purposes.

What God does not do is prevent humanity from using its own powers of domination to inflict pain on itself or on creation. And the urge to dominate runs deep.

No sooner has the story of Noah ended than the story of the tower of Babel begins, surely one of the most relevant parables for our present situation.

The city and tower of Babel are raised by a people who want to make a monument to their own pride. It stretches high into the air so that it can dominate and it is raised by a people who believe in the virtues of a monoculture. They are what Jon Sobrino, the Salvadorean theologian, would identify as the progenitors of imperialism: one language, one culture, one master plan and high monuments to alleged achievement.

And of course, in the process, this urban-based empire has no thought for the environment, the earth, the sanctity of the clouds. It clearly wants to dominate everything.

Is there not something here from the primeval era that is reminiscent of the designs of today's imperialists:

Monoglotism: The belief that all the earth should be English-speaking.

Monoculture: What happens when dependent nations are required to produce one major crop for export because the imperial paymasters do not want to encourage diversification in case it leads to independence.

Monoculturalism: A seduction of indigenous or native cultures to the plastic consumerist cultures as promoted and exemplified by the moguls of Hollywood and the Murdoch press.

Monopolisation: The domination of one major trader in the market place who buys up desirable crops and products from small producers at a price which cares nothing for the welfare of the workers but everything for the profit margin of the trader.

Empires dominate, communities relate; and it is that communitarian, global-village mentality which, if anything, the Bible espouses when it draws humanity into an interactive relationship with its earth habitat.

3) Global warming is a justice issue

It is such because, in the first instance, humanly engineered ecological disaster is unjust to the earth which has regulatory mechanisms in place to deal with temporary imbalances. Hence during natural droughts in Australia some gum trees burst into flame only in order that regeneration can begin.

But if the air is overheated or the ocean over-fished or the sub-continent of South America peppered by mudslides where once forest was, nature is unfairly being asked to cope with what is beyond its capacity for self-adjustment.

A woman with a family of three plus her husband may be able to cope if he brings back a colleague for dinner. She might put more water in the gravy or cut down the portions for the family. But if the husband, who is a football player, decides to bring back the whole team and the opposition, then even the most versatile footballer's wife might find her abilities limited.

We cannot overload creation when its self-correcting mechanism has not been devised to cope with the excesses of human demand or interference.

But a more inhumane effect of global warming, in terms of injustice, is how invariably it is the wealthy who create atmospheric imbalance, but the poor who have to bear the brunt.

The rich will be able for a long while to shore themselves up against the mismanagement of the globe. The Dutch, who have lived below sea-level for a long while, may be able to take appropriate steps to deal with rising waters. Britain, which does not rely on melting snow to fill its reservoirs, is unlikely to suffer from long-term drought this century.

And as long as the USA proliferates nuclear electricity generation, it will be able to keep the humidifiers and air-conditioning units going in cars and homes for another generation.

But what about the poorer coastal nations which cannot build sea walls round their atolls? Or what of land-locked impoverished nations like Nepal where the rivers are already running dry before the glaciers are terminally eroded?

Yet we need not go to the developing world to see the ill effects on the poor of a cavalier approach to environmental integrity.

Peggy Shepard begins an article about the state of public health in New York City with these words:

'The urban ecosystem in West Harlem is typical of the environmental witches' brew found throughout the United States.'

She goes on to cite how, in New York, the North River sewage system has been located on 137th St, next to a poor area. It cost $1.3bn to build, though it provided no work for local unemployed people, and ever since it came into operation it has spewed sickening emissions into the West Harlem Community.

She mentions how disregard for the purity of the air has led to 50% of New York children being at risk of lead poisoning, and notes the high proportion of African American teenagers spread in special education classes because of hyperactivity, which can be a product of lead poisoning.

Sean McDonagh, the Irish Jesuit, puts our dilemma succinctly:

'If the total history of the universe were somehow compressed into a single year, human beings would appear on earth at 11pm on the 365th day. The industrial revolution, which is having such a deleterious impact on the biosphere would take place during the last half-second of the year.'

Yet it is precisely the exploits of neo-imperialism in this half-second which is threatening the 365 days of ecological integrity.

The care of the earth is a justice issue.

4) Love as well as justice

It is also an issue of love, not that the two are necessarily separable. But the love I want to allude to is of neither the romantic nor the sentimental variety. We have had enough of that as regards creation, particularly in the hymnody of the church.

'All things bright and beautiful' might have a good tune, but the words are dangerous if all they do is encourage passive appreciation rather than active conservation.

The love I want to speak of is enshrined in one of the most frequently cited texts from the New Testament. It appears on the majority of those toilet-paper-thin tracts which desperate-looking street evangelists thrust into the hands of unsuspecting shoppers. The kind that have a drawing of the gates of hell and a question in red ink thereunder, such as:

'Do you know where you are going to spend eternity?'

For most shoppers, Sainsbury's or John Lewis might be their preferred – if not biblically appropriate – answer.

On the back of such a tract, you might find this text:

'God so loved the world that he gave his only begotten son that whosoever believeth in him should not perish but have everlasting life.'

What the purveyors of tracts and I suppose many more even-tempered Christians fail to see is that this verse does not take as its starting point either the crucifixion or personal salvation as an alternative to hellfire.

It is a declaration of God's affection: God so loved the world.

And that, in brief, is why Christians have to be concerned about climate change and global warming. Because God loves the world, anything which menaces or threatens what God loves has to be resisted.

I am aware that, thus far, I have alluded primarily to texts in the Hebrew scriptures. The fact that within the New Testament there are far fewer references to care for the earth is not an indication that after Jesus came theological earth science took a back seat.

Christ did not come to annul the law and the prophets and the psalms, he came to fulfil them. His incarnation was not simply for the benefit of humanity. It was to and for the created order he came, of which humanity is a part. And the resurrection which the natural order witnessed happened so that all that was sullied in humanity and by humanity could be redeemed.

As the letter to the Colossians states, it is not *all people* who have been created through Christ, but *'the whole universe'*. It is not *all people* who are reconciled to him through the cross, but *'all things, whether on heaven or on earth'*. (Colossians 1:13-20)

A subjective coda

What I have said so far is fairly objective.

I want to finish on a more personal note about encouraging people to respond to the threat of global warming.

Since the '60s, I have demonstrated and petitioned against a whole range of social and international evils: the Vietnam War, the Falklands War, the possession of nuclear weapons, apartheid in South Africa, the poll tax.

These issues are all intrinsically different from that of global warming on two accounts. Firstly, and certainly as regards anti-apartheid and the nuclear issue, there was an educational job to be done. The public did not know what was happening in South Africa and to what extent Britain was condoning misery. Nor did many people have an idea of what would be the outcome if a nuclear bomb were dropped on either side of the iron curtain.

But there was also a different political perspective. For when one protested against intransigence and for change on any of the above issues, there was always the hope that if only a sufficient number of parliamentarians were persuaded to change their minds, victory would be won, government policy would be reversed and the world would be a safer place.

The issue we are dealing with here is very different.

We do not need to persuade the government of its importance; the British government has shown its awareness. Nor do we have to supply information to an ignorant population. Even the tabloid newspapers regularly publicise the planet's deteriorating state of health.

As regards global warming, we have essentially to persuade ourselves and then others to be less greedy at a time when many of us live in denial of the fact that greediness is a dominant feature of our lifestyle. The earth simply cannot survive if the Western world cavalierly consumes and pollutes at its present rate, thereby setting the standard for others to emulate.

I do not believe we need more research, as ex-President Bush did, nor do I believe we should put all our eggs in the science basket.

For even if science were to produce carbon-neutral fuels, the time it would take for these expensive new commodities to be universally available would be decades. And it would not just be a matter of better fuel. Cars and buses, trains and planes would have to be refitted to use the new fuel, or retired into obsolescence so that brand new vehicles or machines could take the old ones' place. The issue to which we must urgently attend is nothing less than the halting of unbridled hedonism which promotes the pursuit of personal pleasure as the primary human activity.

There is no evidence in history which suggests that when a nation or civilisation grows wealthy and raises its expectations of personal aggrandisement, its subjects will automatically know when enough is enough. Nor is there any historical precedent for believing that unbridled consumerism leads to deep personal fulfilment. Life-threatening decadence is more regularly the outcome.

Because the West and particularly the English-speaking West has taken for itself the mantle of world leadership, it is that same sector of humanity which now, not in some deferred penitential era, must make clear adjustments and sacrifices.

We know what we have to do. Indeed we are almost deaf to the mantras which encourage us *inter alia* to: make fewer journeys by plane, make better use of public ground transportation, make our homes energy-efficient, eat more locally sourced produce, purchase more fairly-traded products, recycle as much waste as possible.

All these things are regularly rehearsed. But they require from each of us active commitment. For unless we show personal willingness to pursue such self-regulated changes, we have no right to pass the buck on to the government, or even worse to expect the developing world to make yet more sacrifices in order that we can enjoy our excesses.

But government and politicians will have to be tough. Britain used to pride itself on how rationing got it through the war. What we are facing, as regards global warming, is something commonly regarded as more menacing than any military or terrorist threat, affecting as it does the survival of the whole world and its populations.

For people of humanitarian instinct and especially those of Christian persuasion, living more simply may be an imperative which they take on voluntarily. But for those whose affluence has for too long gone unchecked, and for corporations whose sophistry knows no bounds when it comes to rationalising excess profits and indulgence, there will have to be legislation to curb industrial and economic practices which exacerbate the problem rather than provide an answer. And parties of the right and left will have to bite this bullet for the good of the globe.

Yet grim statistics and grim warnings are not the best way to defeat that egocentric lust euphemistically called consumerism. What we have to do is to appeal to altruism. That's a very Jesus thing to do, to be driven by the potential of what could happen rather than be immobilised by the magnitude of the problem.

So I end with a cameo of what is probably Britain's first energy-self-sufficient church. I visited it a few years ago.

With the enthusiastic co-operation of the congregation and

local people, the 1846 building was gutted. The pews were replaced with flexible seating for the same number of people. The reappointment of the space inside allowed for vestibule space to limit the effect of cold weather when the doors were open, and double glazing was installed.

A heat pump provides background warmth all year round, and extra electrical demands are met by a wind turbine near the building. It is now open every day to the whole community and has a computer room with four terminals for community access.

Where has this prophetic activity taken place? It happened in one of the most windswept locations in Britain, the island of Westray in the Orkneys.

I sometimes wonder, if a settled community on this remote island can make such a bold and altruistic move, why has it not happened in London?

That is one of a number of enigmas with which people in Scotland have to live. After all, we have the highest concentration of nuclear weapons in Europe cosily tucked up in the Clyde estuary.

Why isn't Trident docked at Canary Wharf if it's so safe?

... but that's another issue.

The beast that is in us

History to which we are inured

There are moments when the truth of history to which we have been inured or about which we have been ignorant begins to worry or even haunt us.

I first recognised this innocence about history in 1978 when, recently licensed to preach, I was dispatched to the Strath of Kildonan in the north-east of Scotland. It is a valley which runs diagonally between Helmsdale and Thurso, a beautiful and bleak landscape, best noted for what is called the Flow Country.

While there for two months, I occasionally hiked on the moorland, and kept coming across the remnants of cottages, disused for who knows how long. It was only when back in the Central Belt (of Scotland) that I enquired of a historian why there were so many disused buildings in a valley which, in places, was very fertile.

And then I learned about the Clearances, a term hitherto unknown to me, even though I had studied history at high school. The term is plural because the phenomenon spanned almost a century, beginning in north-east Scotland in the 1790s and still prevailing in the Western Isles in the 1880s.

Essentially the Clearances involved the forced eviction and expatriation of the rural poor, not because of any crime they had committed, but because their absentee landlords, most of whom were resident in London, realised that their distant territories could earn much more as sheep pasture or as deer forests than as plots for subsistence farming by poor tenants.

The heinous cruelty meted out to innocent people is well recorded in books such as the Canadian historian John

Prebble's *The Highland Clearances* and the lesser known *Mighty as a Lord* written by the Scottish economic historian Ian Fraser Grigor.

It was in the former book that I discovered that the Strath of Kildonan, to which I had been posted and which was home to probably around 200 inhabitants in 1978, had been the habitat for over 2000 people two centuries earlier. Enraged as I was by the cruelty visited on their poorest subjects by nobles waited on by liveried servants 650 miles away, any sense of being distanced from the events was quashed by two gradual revelations.

The first was that the eviction of these illiterate Gaelic-speaking Highlanders was supervised by stewards recruited from the Central Belt, including one Patrick Sellar, a loyal curmudgeon in the service of the Duke and Countess of Sutherland. Lowland Scots were therefore not exempt from blame.

My second shock was with regard to the Presbyterian clergy. For, with the few exceptions of ministers such as Donald Sage of Kildonan and Norman MacLeod, 'the friend of the Gaels', in Fiunary, many Presbyterian ministers not only refused to speak for their parishioners but aided and abetted the evictions by translating the missives from English into Gaelic.

Bad enough as that was, some went further and gave scriptural endorsement to the forced movement of peoples by preaching on selected texts from the Old Testament which they interpreted as intimating God's judgement on lazy and sinful people.

One of the Free Church ministers in the parish of Ross wrote this tragic memorandum about what so often went unchallenged by his clerical colleagues:

'Nothing short of a visit to their quarters and conversation with the poor creatures themselves could give an idea of the misery and wretchedness to which people of this parish are reduced by the heartless and cruel tyranny of their oppressors. Here this is a kind of slavery ten times worse than that which for so long disgraced Britain.'

It does not surprise me when people in the USA and Canada claim to have Scottish ancestry but are unable to prove it. The displaced crofters left for the New World with nothing in their hands and no written proof of their pasts. It is only in baptismal registers of the parishes affected by the Clearances that the possible identification of progenitors might be found.

Another moment of revelation happened in 1981 when I found myself standing in a Bristol Street called White Ladies' Walk, not far distant from another oddly named thoroughfare called Black Boy Hill. The visible connectedness of British cities to the Triangular Trade Route (as it was euphemistically called in our high school history books) had never impressed itself so directly on me. But that was Bristol, not Glasgow.

It took me until 2007 to realise that the Jamaica Bridge, Tobago Street and the more pious-sounding St Vincent Street in Glasgow city centre were not named after favourite holiday venues. Nor were the tobacco and tea merchants celebrated in the city's economic history people renowned for that kind of altruism favoured by more humanitarian businessmen like Robert Owen of New Lanark. Eighteenth-century Glasgow was up to its neck in the slave trade, Jamaica and St Vincent being two islands where Scots owned plantations.

But to sound a positive note, I'd like to allude to an equally unrehearsed historical incident in which some pride might be taken. In his recently published book *Scotland and the Aboli-*

tion of Black Slavery, 1756–1838, Iain Whyte notes that long before Wilberforce had allied himself to the abolitionists' cause, Scottish judges had liberated black men living in Scotland but in the bonded service of Scottish merchants.

One such occasion involved the case of a slave called Joseph Knight who in 1774 appealed to a local magistrate in Perth to rule on his status. The judgement of the Sheriff Depute, John Swinton, found in favour of Knight and four years later this was homologated by an eight-to-four majority in the Court of Session.

The judgement attested:

> 'That the state of slavery is not recognised by the laws of this Kingdom, and is inconsistent with the principles thereof, and finds that the regulations in Jamaica concerning slaves do not extend to this Kingdom, *and repels the master's claim for perpetual service.*'

This, however, does not exonerate my nation from its involvement in slavery, the profits from which erected buildings and estates still in use today.

Other nations and amnesia

Of course, the culture of ignorance or denial about one's history is not restricted to the nations occupying the British Isles.

Small countries in the grip of oligarchies waken up to discover that important moments in their struggle for liberation or liberalisation have been gradually erased from inherited knowledge.

This is what I discovered in El Salvador, to which I went at the invitation of Christian Aid to help produce audio-visual material for one of their campaigns. On the Sunday we were at mass commemorating the 26th anniversary of the assassination of Archbishop Oscar Romero. This took place not in the main sanctuary, but in the crypt of the church. It was led by a dissident priest from Guatemala. Meanwhile, upstairs in the main cathedral building a more sedate celebration was being presided over by Romero's Opus Dei-leaning successor.

Disturbing though that was, a more disquieting incident happened the next day. I was interviewing a 15-year-old boy called Jus, who lived in undoubtedly the poorest house I have ever visited. I mentioned to him that people in my country remembered El Salvador because of the heroic stance of Oscar Romero during the civil war. But Jus seemed oblivious to both the name of the prelate and that damnable externally engineered conflict which ruined his nation.

Later I asked a teacher why such a boy did not know what his country had so recently gone through. She replied that the new education syllabus taught Salvadorean history in the 8th grade, around the age of 14/15, by which time most Salvadorean peasant children have left school.

More recently, I was talking to a girl from another small nation, the Netherlands. I asked her whether there was any period of her nation's recent history that she wished she had been told about. 'Yes,' she immediately replied, and then went on to speak about the period before the invasion of Holland by Germany when the Dutch police collaborated with the enemy.

Her grandfather had been a dissident in Germany and subsequently a refugee in the more humanitarian Netherlands. But, in advance of the invasion, the German army asked the

Dutch police to round up particular people and this man was sent to a concentration camp by the very nation which had agreed to give him shelter.

The battle to keep true history alive is also waged in the world's greatest, or rather only, contemporary superpower. The degree of ignorance which the average American shows about either his or her nation's own history or its present colonial adventures is appalling beyond belief.

I work in the States for up to three months every year. I see the contrast between the USA and its near neighbour Canada whenever I open the newspapers from their respective countries or talk to people about global issues.

In 2007, when in San Francisco, I was amazed to discover that in *The San Francisco Chronicle*, a reputable paper, the amount of coverage given to non-American events amounted to less than one page. Most world coverage deals with where the troops are stationed or where the president visits, plus news about the *World* baseball and *World* ice hockey tournaments, the finals of which usually involve two North American teams playing against each other for the 'global' trophy.

And when it comes to a knowledge of that nation's exploits in Central America, either by direct military intervention or, as in the Nicaraguan civil war, in the form of payments to the USA-backed faction made from public offerings in Southern Baptist churches, few know a fraction of the story.

It may be sufficient to recount a conversation with an American doctor in a restaurant after I had preached in a Manhattan church. We got round, inevitably, to talking about 9/11. It was, after all, within six months of the attack on the twin towers.

In the course of our exchange, I chose my words carefully in saying that '9/11, of course, was not the first time that the territory known as the USA had been attacked'. The doctor looked puzzled, even suspecting himself of premature Alzheimer's. I then mentioned the name Hawaii, and he immediately responded, 'Oh, of course, the Japanese bombing of Pearl Harbour.' 'No,' I said. 'I was actually thinking of the 4th July 1898 when descendants of Protestant missionaries imprisoned Queen Liliuokalani, disabled the police force and effectively annexed a sovereign nation to the USA without plebiscite or consultation with its inhabitants.' This information led the dear doctor to suggest that I had been influenced by Marxism.

When I further mentioned that 9/11 was also the day on which the USA had deposed Salvador Allende, the democratically elected president of Chile, he looked as if he needed to self-medicate for stress.

Why do I say these things?

Because every generation has the right to know the truth about what its predecessors did for good or ill in the world. And the most 'civilised' nations need to guard and disseminate this truth most effectively if their sons and daughters are to fully understand why some nations hate them and others extol them.

Most people of any sensitivity feel outraged when European academics try to deny the holocaust. Fortunately, the Jewish community is both strong and vocal in rehearsing the truth of what has been denied.

But who tells the British about how they parcelled up Palestine and promised an independent country to Jews and Palestinians alike? Who will tell Americans about their ambiguous favouring and threatening of the leaders of Afghanistan and Iraq? Who will remind the world leaders that when the decimation of Tutsis in Rwanda was foreseen by Canadian peacemakers, nobody heeded the cry to prevent the massacre of 800,000 innocents? Who will tell Israeli children about how their nation chooses to assent to the United Nations' mandates on the basis of self-interest rather than international justice? Who will tell white Australians that the so-called Aboriginal 'problem' has more to do with the predatory instincts of white settlers than the presumed indolence and stupidity of people who have walked that land for thousands of years?

There was a time when I thought that Bristol should, out of penitence and respect, eradicate the names of streets whose nomenclature seems so offensive.

I no longer think that way. I believe that White Ladies' Walk and Black Boy Hill should be eliminated from view. I believe they should be called:

> Emancipation Way, formerly known as White Ladies' Walk
> and
> Abolition Crescent, formerly known as Black Boy Hill.

The sorry past to which these street names bear witness is too important to be forgotten, if for no other reason than that which sages have articulated throughout the centuries, namely that the evil we have done, if forgotten, will surely appear again.

I believe that there is, therefore, a genuine responsibility to future generations to be open about the past. For surely, if we try to cover up the wrong that has been done, it gives moral and political precedent for them to follow suit. And in an increasingly interconnected world, we need transparency, not secrecy.

Old phenomena, new reality

The phenomenon of slavery is not solely or primarily an activity of the past. Bold and important coverage has been given to, *inter alia*, the historical practice of slavery in Islamic nations, and the sexual slavery of women from eastern Europe or developing world nations who end up in Western European brothels. There has been exposure of the enslavement of children in African rebel armies and in Asian textile manufacturing industries.

To these I would add a form of slavery not commonly regarded as such – incarceration. The USA has the highest proportion of its inhabitants in penal institutions of any statistically verifiable country in the world, and around 60% of these are African American, despite the fact that this ethnic group amounts to around only 10% of the population.

I could trace the history of black Americans from slavery through the abolition and civil rights movements to the present day and detail an ontology of cruelty which inevitably creates an almost genetic predisposition to low self-esteem, persecution- and inferiority-complexes, and a limited sense of social mobility.

But what I would prefer to do is to reflect on penal practices which, particularly in the USA, continue the pedigree of inhumanity exhibited in the transatlantic slave trade. So much so that one is led to ponder whether there is an ontological and genetic pedigree of cruelty within the American penal psyche.

Colin Dayan is the Robert Penn Professor of Humanities at Vanderbilt University. She recently published a monograph entitled *The Story of the Cruel and Unusual*, which is to some extent a commentary on the USA's use and abuse of the Eighth Amendment.

The Eighth Amendment to the constitution traces its history back to the Bill of Human Rights promulgated in the English parliament of 1689 to greet the accession of William and Mary. The phrase 'cruel and unusual punishments' was incorporated into the American Bill of Rights in 1791 in the laudable sentence:

> *Excessive bail shall not be required,*
> *nor excessive fines imposed,*
> *nor cruel and unusual punishments inflicted.*

For the last two centuries, the USA has seen a remarkable range of judicial eggheads outdoing each other's sophistry in an attempt to reinterpret that phrase permissibly so that gross acts of degradation and inhumanity authorised at the highest level are largely unrestricted.

The horrors of Abu Ghraib and Guantanamo Bay would not have been permitted in most westernised countries. But in the USA, legislators have ensured that what the civilised world deems brutal and inhumane is sanctioned. Cases of psychological cruelty inflicted on inmates have been dismissed because there were no physical marks of long-term injury. And where brutal physical treatment has been meted out without just cause, it has been deemed to fall short of the ever-changing understanding of 'cruel and unusual punishments'.

Thus, in Guantanamo in 2003 alone, there were 350 recorded acts of self-harm, which included individual and mass suicide attempts. The response to such events was not to question why there should be such a high rate of self-harm, but to find means of discouraging it. One such was inflicted on 131 men during a large hunger strike in 2006. They were strapped to chairs while coloured tubes were inserted through their noses to enable force-feeding, an unimaginably excruciating experience.

Commenting on this practice, General John Craddock, then head of the US Southern Command, said:

> 'It's not like the Chair. It's *a* chair. It's pretty comfortable. It's not abusive.'

In June of the same year, three detainees committed suicide. Their lawyers said they had hanged themselves in despair. Showing that high-ranking American affection for Orwellian linguistic transubstantiation, Rear Admiral Henry Harris, the camp commander, commented that the dead men ...

> 'had no regard for life, either ours or their own. I believe that this was not an act of desperation, but an act of asymmetrical warfare waged against us.'

But lest we imagine that such atrocities are the preserve of military detention centres, it might be appropriate to cite a rare instance of a judgement in favour of an imprisoned plaintiff in a 'normal' state penitentiary. I refer to a case in 1995 when Chief Judge Thelton Henderson condemned the habits of the Pelican Bay prison whose penal treatments included:

> 'The caging of inmates outdoors in freezing temperatures

... the unnecessary and sometimes lethal force used in removing an inmate from his cell

'... the scalding of a mentally disabled black inmate, burned so badly that from his buttocks down the skin peeled off, while an officer standing by mocked, "Looks like we're going to have a white boy before this is through."'

If Britain had the low rates of imprisonment and recidivism found in other EU countries, we might look contemptuously on the penal practices of the USA. But our hands are not clean. Physical brutality of warders towards inmates is certainly not as prevalent as across the Atlantic, but the failure to engage constructively with incarcerated people destines many of them to the bondage of re-offending and re-imprisonment.

I say this from a little personal involvement.

For the past eight years I have corresponded continuously with an inmate of a Scottish prison. His name is Gary. He was put away for 12 years, aged 16, for involvement in armed robbery. Prior to this he had effectively been removed from civil society since the age of eight. He saw his mother raped and he himself was raped by his grandfather. He also, on two occasions, found his mother about to hang herself. His aberrant behaviour in state school led to his being educated in a more restrictive facility.

After 10 years of imprisonment and with absolutely no training for freedom he was told one day that he was being given a week out on licence. He was given a return ticket from a prison in Perthshire to Glasgow and £15.00. No attempt had been made to establish whether a former prison chaplain who had offered to accommodate him on release would be around on the day when, without warning, he was released on licence. He phoned to ask if he could get a taxi to my house and stay there until he could make contact with his longer-term host. I met him off the train, a young man dressed in ill-fitting clothes which did not belong to him, suddenly set loose in a city he did not know. Had he put a £5.00 note in the money box of a local bus, he would be unaware that there was no possibility of getting any change for a 50p ride.

He was let out of prison on four occasions, and returned behind bars fairly quickly on all but the last. This was not because he was stupid or of an innate criminal disposition. In simple terms, he had nowhere that was home. He was released into a neighbourhood rife with drug abuse and ended up being involved in petty crime to feed a habit he had not had in prison.

When I asked him why he was associating with junkies, he said,

> 'The community of drug users is the only group of people who will accept me.'

This young man was probably the most intellectually talented individual I ever met. On one occasion two years ago, when I asked him what books he'd like me to bring back from the USA, he asked for the combined volumes of Karl Barth's *Church Dogmatics*. He could cite Greek and Hebrew etymology with flawless accuracy despite having been effectively removed from mainstream education at the age of eight.

Only on the fourth occasion when he was released was he enabled to go into supported accommodation for homeless men. There, with encouragement from the staff, he began to thrive, and to make plans for further education.

One of the saddest moments in my life was being told that, the day after I had spoken to him on the phone and had arranged for him to buy new clothes, he was found dead in his bedroom. There were no suspicious circumstances.

Throughout the British Isles and irrespective of political administrations, the prevailing wisdom has been to increase the prison population, oblivious to the proven fact that prisons criminalise offenders rather than reform them, and equally oblivious to the need, if the prison population expands and more punishable offences end up on the statute book, for increased staffing to supervise parole and probation.

It is a highly reprehensible indictment of our 'civilised' society to discover Dr Andrew McLellan, Her Majesty's Chief Inspector of Prisons (Scotland), criticising the detention of children under 16 years of age in rooms in certain penal institutions for up to 23 hours per day.

This is the new slavery of which most of us know so little.

I entitled this talk *The beast that is within us*, taking that phrase from William Golding's novel *Lord of the Flies*, in which a group of boys marooned in a remote location gradually come to terms with how the evil which they attribute to malign powers around them is actually self-generated.

Slavery was not and is not a system imposed by demonic powers on innocent humanity. It is a system that is chosen, engineered and, to some extent, enjoyed by human beings.

And, though we might wish it were otherwise, I want to suggest that slavery has as much to do with race as rape has to do with sex. Both are primarily exhibitions of sadistic dominant force used against unwilling victims.

Ground conditions encouraging slavery

So I want, in closing, to identify some of the preconditions for practices of the same genre as slavery which are as prevalent and sometimes as socially sanctioned in the present as in the past. Please note that these are only some of the contributing factors and will not all necessarily be operative in every case.

Following each issue, I will indicate the contra flow of the Gospel as exhibited in Jesus of Nazareth.

1) The sanction of religion

This enabled the expulsion of Highlanders from their native shores in the 19th century. It also enabled the forced migration of millions of black Africans.

It was not simply that the Church of England owned slave-plantations in the West Indies, that plantation owners and slave ports had chaplains who always endorsed and never challenged the barbarities they witnessed. It is not simply that, contrary to popular opinion, John Newton's hymn Amazing Grace had nothing to do with his social enlightenment. (The song was written about an internal spiritual awakening after which he continued to captain slave ships, hold services for the crew on deck while the slaves languished below, and attribute his good fortune and pleasant occupation to the grace of God.)

No, slavery, like apartheid, was given scriptural warrant by sectors of Christendom who needed to find a divine mandate to sanction their vilest impulses.

When I worked in South Africa in 2004-5, I was privileged to speak with both black and white scholars and preachers about the misuse of the Bible, to discover how the primitive story of Noah cursing a son for looking on his nakedness was taken to be a warrant for divine censure of the negro races which all good Christians had to endorse. Furthermore, the story of the Tower of Babel was understood as an indication that separate development (apart-heid) was a divinely ordained institution and punishment. In contrast, a liberationist reading would see difference as part of God's glorious purpose.

And what about all those texts from the Pauline epistles which seem to condone slavery, texts over which the Methodist church and other denominations in the USA sweated and eventually tore themselves in two, as keenly as Anglicans are doing today on the issue of homosexuality, despite that issue having a much lower biblical profile.

How would it have felt to be a slave sitting in the gallery of a Presbyterian church in Georgia when the epistle was read which said, 'Slaves, obey your masters'? For such texts were wont to be followed by a sermon to drive home the fact of slavery as a divine ordinance without ever the attempt to distinguish between bonded service in the 1st-century Roman Empire and the 18th-century transportation of black Africans across the Atlantic.

Of course, such perverting of scripture happened without recourse to the Gospel, in which Jesus continually identifies in the marginalised gifts he does not perceive among the safe or the saved. Nor would reference ever be made to the solidarity of the black man who carried Jesus' cross, or the black indigenous church which began when the apostle Philip baptised a eunuch.

2) The commodification of beings

The theology of a previous day helped both slave-owners and the architects and upholders of apartheid to regard black people as sub-human, a species apart. Slaves were the second cargo on the triangular trade route, less valuable than tobacco or sugar, able to be sold for a price or jettisoned during a storm. Like coffee and cotton, slaves were not considered to have a place of belonging or a notion of their destiny. Though animate, they were treated if not as lifeless then certainly as meaningless.

Which is exactly the way, as Colin Dayan describes, the American penal system sees inmates. Let me quote her on what she calls the 'domain of corrections'.

> 'Though many of those incarcerated in state prisons in the United States are not violent offenders, they are exposed to the most public degradation, warehoused indefinitely *(note the language of commodity)*, put to work on chain gangs, attacked by dogs, shackled to walls, shocked with tasers. Prisoners' crimes no longer explain their treatments. Society is inventing the criminal, creating a new class of the condemned.'

The very word 'degrading' is a term which essentially lessens the rank of a particular commodity. It can also be used of someone who, for whatever reason, finds their status in the workplace diminished. The kind of thing that happens when a company 'rationalises'. But when used of a person's selfhood, *de-grading* means losing the status of being considered human.

So, Dayan cites the experience of prisoners:

> 'Inmates have described life in their massive, windowless, super-maximum prisons as akin to "living in a tomb",

"circling in space", "being freeze-dried".'

When we talk about prison numbers increasing, we should be aware that we are sanctioning the rhetoric of slavery. It is not numbers that increase. Numbers are inanimate. It is people who become more numerous, whether in slave plantations or in so-called correctional facilities.

When people talk about the black problem, or the prison problem, or the immigration problem, there is a similar linguistic confusion. Colours, institutions and policies are inanimate. The issue is human lives, each one made in the image of the living God. And we constantly have to guard against the temptation to reify human beings, to turn every he and she into an it, a commodity.

It is not the kettle that boils, but the water in it. It is not prisons or detention centres which are a problem. The problem lies with the allegedly law-abiding majority who cannot deal with the personhood of people who are unlike them.

How lovely that Jesus refuses to reify, to see people as things or as problems. How lovely that he takes the 'problem' of a crippled woman and gives her a title: 'She is a daughter of Abraham.'

How lovely when he makes the leper 'problem' into a community resource. The ten leprous men whom he heals are sent to the priest to be revalidated as participating citizens in their locality.

How lovely when Jesus refuses to enter into a philosophical discussion with Pilate about the abstract nature of truth, but confronts him with a person to whom Pilate can, if he wishes, relate.

Indeed, is the incarnation not essentially about God refusing to be reified, but rather taking a human face, in order that all human faces might own their dignity?

3) Addiction to gain

This is what enabled the 'beast in them' to seduce otherwise decent people in the United Kingdom to become willing participants in the global slave trade. The aggrandisement of Bristol, Liverpool and my beloved Glasgow, the fine buildings, the concert halls and museums endowed by philanthropists, the burgeoning ship and manufacturing industries, many of these owed their origin to the lucrative trade in human beings.

I quote Iain Whyte:

> 'For those without capital, the West Indies provided job opportunities ... For those without specific qualifications, the management needs of plantations were an outlet, often a raft, on which to cling in the sea of unemployment ...' (p61)

And if this is indicative of how the slave trade helped the poor and illiterate, how much more did it do for the educated?

Here's Iain Whyte again:

> 'Many [medical graduates] were prepared to combine commercial enterprises with medicine. William Stephen in St Kitts bought sick slaves, treated them and resold them at a profit ...' (p49)

And for the moneyed, slavery could be a goldmine.

'Starved of commercial success for so long, the nation [Scotland] welcomed this economic miracle in which trade associated with slaves and slavery played an important role ... For this reason, men such as Oswald and Grant [Glasgow traders] had no hesitation in including on their coats of arms a black slave, thus openly acknowledging the source of their wealth. (p64)

(Scots, we should remember, owned 30% of the estates in Jamaica)

Ditto with the slavery known as apartheid. Ditto also with wage slavery, as is increasingly witnessed in the faked surprise expressed by clothing importers and retailers when it is exposed how goods produced in India or Sri Lanka or El Salvador require child labour and a pittance of pay to ensure the maximisation of profits for those who sell clothes at low prices in Britain.

And the prison system is not immune to the allure of gain. I wish I could cite the book in which I read this. But when you hand a book in to a prisoner, you cannot always get it back. So I am relying on my memory of a book I gave to Gary which was written by the crime correspondent of *The New York Times*.

He discovered that far from Americans disliking prisons, they love them. Rural towns plead to have a penitentiary nearby. For, as with the slave trade, it provides work for the unskilled who may become prison officers. It provides work for the service industries who maintain its infrastructure. And, *inter alia*, a prison contract is avidly sought by phone companies, because prisoners can only phone out using cards, the most expensive means for the caller and the most lucrative for the wholesaler.

Are we aware that the Christian Gospel encourages the most materialistic of world faiths, and that Jesus talked continuously about money? Witness the parables of the good Samaritan, the prodigal son, Dives and Lazarus, the lost coin, the treasure in the field, the labourers in the marketplace, the talents entrusted to servants.

And this is not by way of censure or condemnation. Having outlined elsewhere the negative lure of money and the shallow life of dependence on the profit margin, Jesus spoke about the good that money could do when used altruistically rather than selfishly. When used to liberate rather than incarcerate.

It is in his teaching and in his engagement with the privileged that we see clearly the irony that otherwise evades us. It is the Pharisees, who say that they know everything about the blind man's case, who are told that they actually are the ones who can't see.

It is those who would be quick to incarcerate, enslave or condemn others in order to protect their wealth who are exposed as being in bondage to their own fortune.

4) The lack of a compelling alternative vision

People are led as much by images of what might be as by analysis of what is. It is pointless simply to say that this or that practice is wrong unless there is an alternative possibility which can be envisioned.

And here we have, almost of necessity, to move out of the realms of the secular into those of the sacred or at least the prophetic. But when our personal well-being, and more particularly our smugness, is dependent on the civil endorsement of a corrupt system, it is a threat when we are asked to think or live out of the box.

It is then that we realise that we are like the paralysed man who, when offered healing, found it so uncomfortable to move from unhealthy dependence to self-sufficiency that he went to the authorities to report Jesus who had enabled him to get better.

How do you persuade the world's greatest superpower that, rather than dominate the world, it should become just another player in the global economy? How do you persuade drivers who insist on privately chauffeuring their children to school that it would be better for the environment and for their children if they used public transport?

How do you persuade a nation which has swallowed the myths about the need to incarcerate to believe that there are better alternatives to prison for many people?

Well, sometimes the prophetic action or vision works, as in the case of a man called Les whom I met at Tatamagouche in Nova Scotia.

He decided to start a 'walking bus'. So, with the approval of the local high school, he goes once a week to the periphery of the town and walks for 40 minutes to the school and as many adolescents as wish walk to school with him. They talk to each other, they exercise their limbs and they discover that their mothers' or fathers' cars are not indispensable and do indeed guzzle too much gas.

And there are experiments, as in Australia, where people who have been the victims of crime can choose to have the perpetrator of the crime sentenced (punitive justice) or be engaged in a programme to reform their behaviour (restorative justice). In the latter case, it is not just that the criminal and the victim meet, but they also work out a way of making reparation based on relationship and interaction, thus often leading to the rehumanisation of someone who has been reified.

And there was Martin Luther King who is remembered for a speech he never intended to make. 'I have a dream' was not in his script. It was what Mahalia Jackson urged him to reveal when he had come to the end of a prepared speech. And it was that improvised re-envisioning of the future that compelled and propelled the civil rights movement forward.

So Jesus doesn't theorise much. Unlike Paul, he tells stories about forgiving fathers, and spendthrift party-givers, and marginalised heroes, in order that we who are the victims of the empire might glimpse the kingdom.

5) Self-delusion

If there is a fifth precondition for unyoking 'the beast that is in us', it's the erroneous belief that there is no such thing.

I am sure that some of the worst offenders in the slave trades of the past and the present are within themselves people who believe that what is properly regarded as a vice is actually a virtue. And I have no doubt that many of those in the past or present who support, endorse and vote for a variety of slaveries suffer from the same myopia of the soul.

Hence, in the post-apartheid era the Truth and Reconciliation Commission headed by Archbishop Tutu almost never got off the ground. He wanted it to involve all sectors of the community. The blacks and coloureds were keen on Truth and Reconciliation. The whites wanted Reconciliation without hearing the Truth. Many still believed, despite the judgement of the world, that in their corporate vice there was collective virtue.

So Christ does not allow us to have resurrection without crucifixion. Nor does he speak of the misery of the cross without the liberation of the empty grave.

Footnote

We are right to celebrate the 200th anniversary of the parliamentary bill proposing the abolition of slavery. But we should be not be presumptive of its total demise when several of its preconditions still are alive and well.

Despite a half-century of liberation theology, populist Christian theologians are keen to find biblical sanction for avarice and fail to draw on deeper spiritual wells to undergird the combating of racism, neo-colonialism and ecological devastation.

Despite the rallying cries about the sanctity of the unborn and the desire of the White House that 'no child be left behind', when it comes to child poverty in the USA or the UK, playing with statistics can sometimes be a displacement activity that avoids dealing with the real issue which is people, not things.

Despite every indication, from the obesity rate to the state of the banks, that unbridled consumption and the lust for gain bring a trail of disasters in their wake, we are more convinced by the allure of private capital than the potential of social capital.

And when it comes to dreams and visions, the silence of

prophetic voices in politics is matched only by their corresponding absence in the Church.

Bertolt Brecht has a very interesting play entitled *The Resistible Rise of Alberto Ui*. It charts the rise to power of Adolf Hitler as paralleled in the more localised but equally malevolent ascendancy of Al Capone.

I remember seeing it in London when I was 18. It was a magnificent performance, memorable for the amazing stage effect when, right at the end, Ui stood on a hydraulic platform draped in red and black. As it gradually rose from the stage into the auditorium, he addressed the theatre audience as if we were his fascist aficionados.

As the speech, reminiscent of the Nuremberg rallies, ended and the stage faded to darkness, lines were projected, of which I can only remember the last:

'The bitch that bore him is still in heat.'

Delivered at Sarum College, 2nd Nov 2007

Works cited:
The Story of the Cruel and the Unusual by Colin Dayan. MIT Press, 2007.
Scotland and the Abolition of Black Slavery, 1756–1838 by Iain Whyte. Edinburgh University Press, 2006.

The Wild Goose Resource Group

The Wild Goose Resource Group is an expression of the Iona Community's commitment to the renewal of public worship. Based in Glasgow, the WGRG has three resource workers, John Bell and Graham Maule and Jo Love, who lead workshops, seminars and events throughout Britain and abroad. They are supported by Gail Ullrich (administrator) and Karen Turner (sales administrator).

From 1984 to 2001, the WGRG workers were also part of the Wild Goose Worship Group. The WGWG consisted of around sixteen, predominantly lay, people at any one time, who came from a variety of occupational and denominational backgrounds. Over the 17 years of its existence, it was the WGWG who tested, as well as promoted, the material in this book.

The task of both groups has been to develop and identify new methods and materials to enable the revitalisation of congregational song, prayer and liturgy. The songs and liturgical material have now been translated and used in many countries across the world as well as being frequently broadcast on radio and television.

The WGRG, along with a committed group of fellow-Glaswegians, run HOLY CITY, a monthly ecumenical workshop and worship event for adults in the centre of Glasgow. The WGRG also publishes a mail-order catalogue, an annual Liturgy Booklet series and a twice-yearly newsletter, GOOSEgander, to enable friends and supporters to keep abreast of WGRG developments. If you would like to find out more about subscribing to these, or about ways to support the WGRG financially, please contact:

The Wild Goose Resource Group, Iona Community, Fourth Floor, Savoy House, 140 Sauchiehall Street, Glasgow G2 3DH, Scotland. Tel: 0141 332 6343   Fax: 0141 332 1090   e-mail: wgrg@iona.org.uk web: www.wgrg.co.uk   www.holycity-glasgow.co.uk

WGRG (Facebook):
http://www.facebook.com/group.php?gid=57677125210&ref=ts WGRG (Twitter): http://twitter.com/WildGooseRG

Holy City (Facebook):
http://www.facebook.com/group.php?gid=5675774949&ref=ts Holy City (Twitter): http://twitter.com/HolyCityGlasgow